FROM MISSOURI LIFE
SAVOR
Missouri
RIVER HILL COUNTRY
Food & Wine

By
Nina Furstenau

Photography By
Nina Furstenau & Sarah Herrera

Forewords by
Katie Steele Danner
Director, Missouri Division of Tourism

and

Jon Hagler
Director, Missouri Department of Agriculture

Missouri Life
THE SPIRIT OF DISCOVERY

501 High Street, Ste. A
Boonville, Missouri 65233
660-882-9898
www.MissouriLife.com

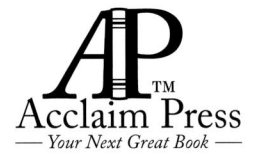

Acclaim Press
— Your Next Great Book —

P.O. Box 238
Morley, MO 63767
(573) 472-9800
www.acclaimpress.com

Book and Cover Design: Kimberly M. Paul

Copyright @ 2013 Nina Furstenau and Missouri Life, Inc.
All Rights Reserved.

No part of this book shall be reproduced or transmitted in any form or by any means, electronic or mechanical, including photocopying, recording or by an information or retrieval system, except in the case of brief quotations embodied in articles and reviews, without the prior written consent of the publisher. The scanning, uploading, and distribution of this book via the Internet or via any other means without permission of the publisher is illegal and punishable by law.

The information from websites of the businesses listed in this book have been used with permission of their respective owners. Other contributing photographers were Nina Bolka, Nate Furstenau, Kaitlin Steinberg, and Greg Wood. Some photographs have been supplied courtesy of the destinations.

Library of Congress Control Number: 2012034852

ISBN-13: 978-1-938905-08-7
ISBN-10: 1-938905-08-3

First Printing: 2013
Printed in the United States of America
10 9 8 7 6 5 4 3 2 1

This book was accuracy checked before printing, but the publisher is not responsible for errors or omissions. Recipes in this book were offered by the featured farms, restaurants, wineries, and businesses.

Note to Reader:

This book is not meant to be comprehensive, but rather to provide a selection of quality Missouri flavors in the River Hills Region, and ones we can heartily endorse. Join in the fun and make your own trip to the area and uncover surprises along the way.

The features in this book are arranged by rivers: the Missouri, the Meramec, and the Mississippi above and below St. Louis, and alphabetically within their area. Single out a town, or visit them all as you can. The region is worth a look and a linger.

The features and contact information were up to date at the time of publication. However, websites, phone numbers, emails, and hours may change. We recommend checking websites or phoning before you travel far to visit the farms, restaurants, and other places featured.

Know someone who should be included? Send your idea for future updates to nfurstenau@gmail.com with the subject line Savor Mo Query.

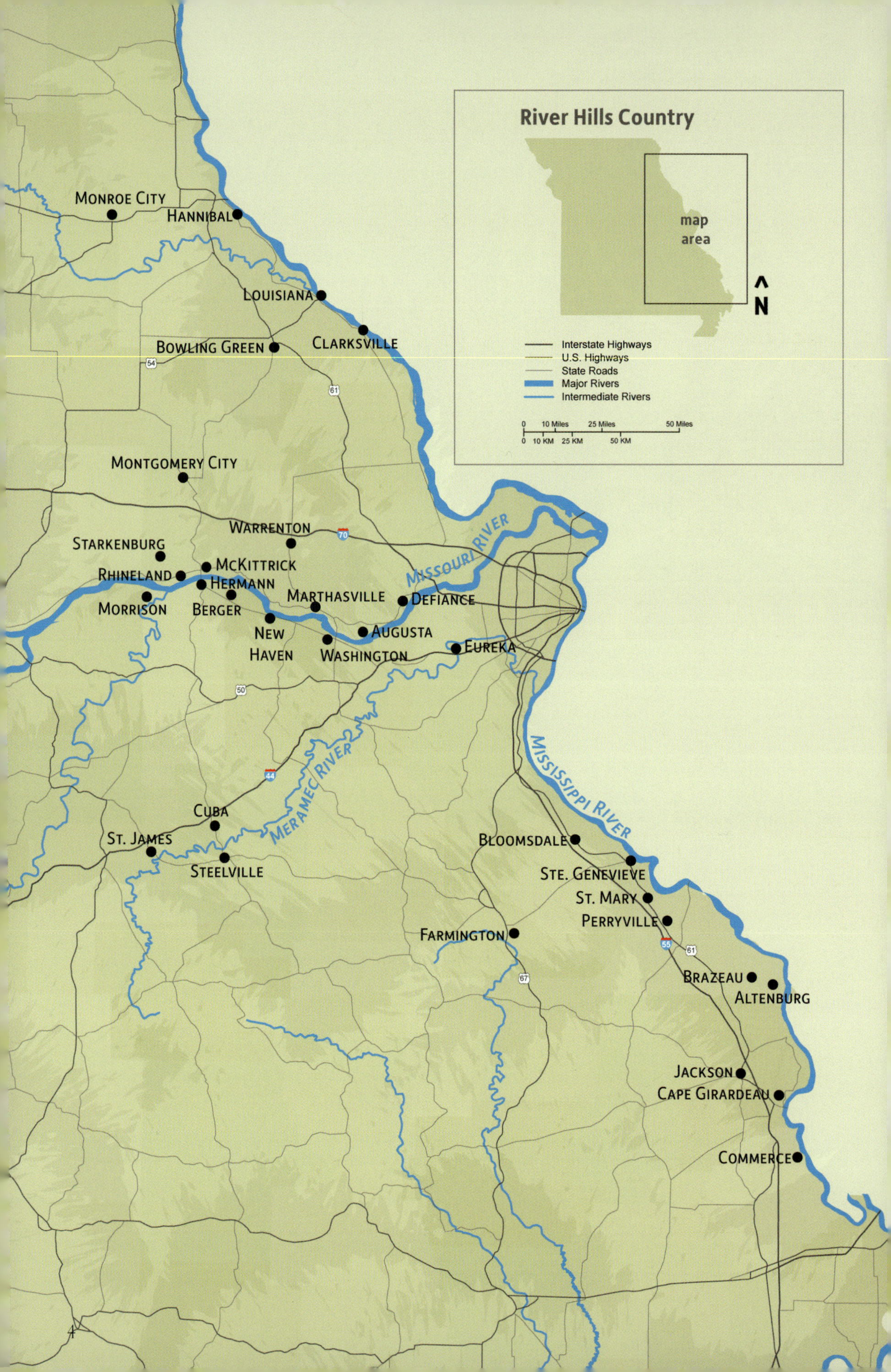
River Hills Country
map area
N
Interstate Highways
U.S. Highways
State Roads
Major Rivers
Intermediate Rivers
0 10 Miles 25 Miles 50 Miles
0 10 KM 25 KM 50 KM
Monroe City
Hannibal
Louisiana
Bowling Green
Clarksville
Montgomery City
Warrenton
Starkenburg
McKittrick
Rhineland
Hermann
Morrison
Berger
Marthasville
Defiance
New Haven
Augusta
Washington
Eureka
Missouri River
Meramec River
Mississippi River
Cuba
St. James
Steelville
Bloomsdale
Ste. Genevieve
St. Mary
Perryville
Farmington
Brazeau
Altenburg
Jackson
Cape Girardeau
Commerce
54
61
70
50
44
55
67

CONTENTS

Foreword by Katie Steele Danner 6
Foreword by Jon Hagler 7
Introduction 8

The Meramec River Hills .... [map, p. 10]
    Cuba 12
    Eureka 16
    St. James 18
    Steelville 22

The Mississippi River Hills
North of St. Louis .... [map, p. 24]
    Bowling Green 26
    Clarksville 32
    Hannibal 34
    Louisiana 40
    Monroe City 46
    Montgomery City 48

The Mississippi River Hills
South of St. Louis .... [map, p. 50]
    Altenburg 52
    Benton 54
    Bloomsdale 56
    Brazeau 58
    Cape Girardeau 60
    Commerce 70
    Farmington 72
    Jackson 74
    Perryville 80
    Ste. Genevieve 84
    St. Mary 98

The Missouri River Hills .... [map, p. 100]
    Augusta 102
    Berger 116
    Defiance 122
    Hermann 124
    Marthasville 144
    McKittrick 146
    Morrison 148
    New Haven 152
    Starkenburg 158
    Warrenton 160
    Washington 162

Acknowledgments 170
Index 172

Foreword

Every recipe has a story.
Really good recipes create stories spanning lifetimes.

With that in mind, consider *Savor Missouri* more than a book from which to create your next meal. Think of it as a gateway to memories your family and friends can share for generations to come.

In Missouri, we're fortunate to have access to many wonderful resources that contribute to memorable meals. We're also fortunate to have a strong agricultural community from which to draw those resources.

From farmers to vintners, these are the people who work hard and get their hands dirty so we can sit down to clean our plates. These are the people that ensure we have fresh products to feed our bodies—and in some cases, nurture our souls.

As you page through *Savor Missouri*, highlight recipes you think you'll enjoy and take time to learn about the people whose stories are shared here. Don't stop there, though.

Get out, explore the Show-Me State, and meet the folks you read about. Like the state itself, they are fun, interesting, and unique.

And, like any good recipe, they're sure to have a story.

Happy reading – and dining,

Katie Steele Danner
Director, Missouri Division of Tourism

VisitMo.com
800-519-4800
for additional travel information

Foreword

JEREMIAH W. (JAY) NIXON
GOVERNOR

**DEPARTMENT *of* AGRICULTURE
STATE OF MISSOURI
JEFFERSON CITY**
*Serving, promoting and protecting the agricultural producers, processors
and consumers of Missouri's food, fuel and fiber products.*

DR. JON HAGLER
DIRECTOR

As Director of the Missouri Department of Agriculture, I have been fortunate to see nearly every mile of this beautiful state. From the Bootheel in the south to the far-reaching corners of the north, there are cornfields for miles and rows of soybeans that seem to go on forever. Herds of horses or cattle find shelter beneath the canopy of the forested Ozark Mountains, and fertile soil throughout our state provides an abundance of crops and produce. Moreover, along the banks of the Missouri River, hidden in the valleys that rest near the horizon, lies one of our best kept secrets, Missouri Wine Country.

Missouri's wine industry has a rich tradition that dates back more than 150 years. German immigrants who settled in Missouri began making wine as early as 1850, and prior to Prohibition our wine industry ranked No. 2 in the country. Our state grape, the Norton, once saved the ravaged wine countries of Europe in the early 1870s. Europe was enduring a Phylloxera epidemic at the time, and because the Norton variety is resistant to the pest, scientists grafted Norton rootstocks onto the vines in Europe. Today, Missouri wine has developed into a complex, rich, and indeed, a thriving industry vital to the success of our state. Missouri is now home to 121 registered wineries, seven wine trails, and 1,600 acres of grapes that produce more than 900,000 gallons of wine a year—a perfect complement to our agricultural abundance.

Perhaps you'll be lucky enough to experience the camaraderie of a hog roast dinner on a perfect Sunday evening, or enjoy a plate of home-smoked beef brisket, sweet corn, hand-snapped peas, and of course a glass of Missouri wine. With this wonderful guide, you can take the time to fully engage your senses, pair these recipes with travel throughout the state, and enjoy all the beauty and tastes this great state has to offer.

Dr. Jon Hagler
Missouri Director of Agriculture

GEORGE WASHINGTON CARVER STATE OFFICE BUILDING
Ph. (573)751-4211 • 1616 Missouri Boulevard • P.O. Box 630 • Jefferson City, MO 65102-0630 • FAX (573) 751-1784 • mda.mo.gov

Introduction

I often drive back roads in Missouri squinting at my map or the directions I've jotted down to get to small farms, centennial orchards, or a family restaurant. The destination is in my mind as I go, winding through hills, trees, and under ribbons of flounced white clouds. Missouri is a place you can do that, pass immeasurable beauty, little remarked, to reach somewhere else. Red barns scuffed by time, quirky houses marked with the ingenuity of using leftover farm detritus as doors or wall fragments, heavily wooded copses and meticulously rowed crop land, it all meets your eyes and recedes. But stopping will get you hooked. Pick a road and brake as you see fit.

This is a book for wanderers. No doubt you will find your own treasures by stopping willy-nilly at beautiful spots, curious roadside restaurants, and seductive wineries calling out with the fruit of the vine and the views. Wind alongside one of our great rivers as I did: the Mississippi, the Missouri, the Meramec, and smaller tributaries leading south. I guarantee that you will see and taste the heartland. There is history to note in every curve of the land, every twist of the road, every bend of the river. There are so many rushing waterways here in Missouri; they refresh the land, add bounty to our tables, transport the produce to mix food cultures on the plate. Have for years.

In fact, if you look at Missouri's food story, you will find the world. There's southern corn bread; German sausage; Italian, French, and German wine-making traditions. There are occasional French, Cajun, and Creole influences coming back upstream, too: little pools of culture and eddies of tradition alongside each of our rivers. Those same rivers and the soils supporting them drive our food trails.

Near Hermann, the sloping hillsides and shallow soils not only reminded German settlers of home, but suited the abundant grapes grown there. The narrow band of hills along the Mississippi makes it difficult to cultivate row crops, and today many small farmers, emerging wineries, and meat producers flourish.

Inland, you will be smitten with the orchards in this state, fewer now than in years past, and the fresh produce stands with thick bunches of kale, of collard, or spinach, their bins beckoning with the fresh seasonal foods that look so beautiful on the plate. The families that have cured meats for generations, the goose lady of Morrison, the Sederwalls of Hannibal who bake breads and treats will all take you on a journey in regional flavor: surprising, tasty, and local. The story of our region is in their work.

Savor Missouri: River Hills Country Food & Wine is focused on the eastern reaches of our state. Think of St. Louis as a hub and visualize spokes of rivers: food and wine lover's spots-to-stop along the Missouri River west to Morrison, the Mississippi north to Hannibal as well as south to Cape Girardeau, and the Meramec River southwest to St. James. I skipped our urban centers and inquired about the favorite local tastes in rural areas wanting, I suppose, a return to our region through its food-ways. Our honey, beef, produce, wine, storied recipes, and more come to us from family-run farms, orchards, restaurants, and wineries that are not necessarily in heavily populated places. Our land, worked by dedicated families through the years, is itself the story. Our place, the products that come of it, are close to hand. Unbelievably so, and the families that live Missouri's story in food or wine production want more than ever to

Louisiana, Missouri

keep their lifestyle viable. It's a lifestyle worth noting, lovely to be a part of if only for a short stop, and welcoming at every turn. Visit this masterpiece of American life. Enjoy with me the idea that we can keep it alive with the support of our taste buds.

The River Hills is a large, rolling region, full of wonderful people doing what they love, sometimes grudgingly during rainstorms or insect invasions, but work they wouldn't trade. I felt privileged to join them for an afternoon or a morning amongst all the work they accomplish each day. The welcome I received was always warm. What a privilege to taste the fruit of their labor: Missouri maple syrup at the Gihrings, fresh cherry pie (nothing better on earth) at Thierbach Orchards, fermented Italian sausage at Williams Bros.

I hope you will take a day trip out, or better still, a three- or four-day trip out into our beautiful River Hills. Our river history, food culture, and wine heritage all meet at the table. Don't miss these connections: take a breath and pick a road. Any road.

Nina Furstenau

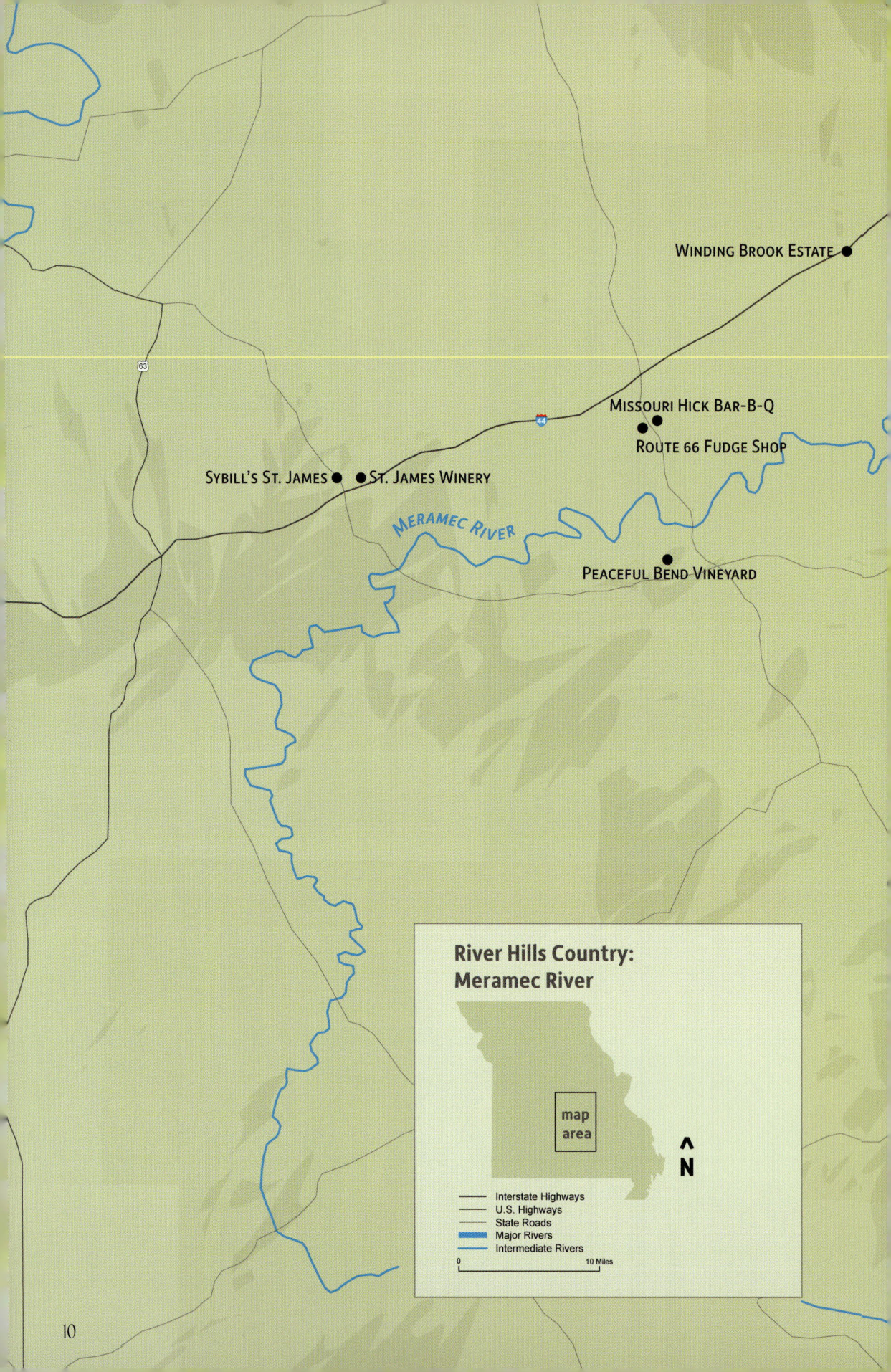

River Hills Country: Meramec River

- Winding Brook Estate
- Missouri Hick Bar-B-Q
- Route 66 Fudge Shop
- Sybill's St. James
- St. James Winery
- Peaceful Bend Vineyard

Meramec River

Legend:
- Interstate Highways
- U.S. Highways
- State Roads
- Major Rivers
- Intermediate Rivers

0 – 10 Miles

Meramec River Hills

MISSOURI HICK BAR-B-Q
CUBA

Cucumber-Onion Salad
Recipe from Fern Meiser; serves 6-8

1 pint white vinegar
1 pint red wine vinegar
2-½ cups water
2-½ cups sugar
4 large cucumbers
4 large red onions

Mix the vinegars, water, and sugar in a bowl and set aside. Score the cucumbers lengthwise with a fork and then slice in ⅛-inch rounds. Cut the onions in half and then slice thinly. Add to the vinegar mixture and serve.

Find smoky meats and Missouri cedar at Missouri Hick Bar-B-Q.

If you like handcrafted wood, you'll love Missouri Hick Bar-B-Q in Cuba. Owner Dennis Meiser came from a family of carpenters but didn't think he fit the mold. Then, he began working with Missouri Eastern Red Cedar, and you can see the results in his building for barbecue. Handmade tables and chairs, a water wheel, and a beautiful staircase showcase the lovely lines of cedar and give the restaurant an invitingly rustic ambience.

The meats are slow cooked here, at least 12 hours, after Dennis applies his special rub. He offers tomato-based sauces that are sweet, spicy, smoky, and combinations of those, as well as a Carolina-style mustard barbecue sauce. The kitchen goes through 64,000 pounds of pork a year, 9,600 slabs of ribs, plus the chicken, brisket, and other beef needed to serve customers. Extra large potatoes are stacked with baked beans, pulled pork, smoky sweet sauce, bacon bits, chives, and two kinds of cheese and special seasonings. Other side dishes range from a dry, tangy German potato salad to baked sweet potatoes, slaw, and more.

It's a popular stop. In fact, to serve expanding business, Dennis opened a Steelville location in late spring 2012 where he offers more grilled options with the barbecue as well as his own line of artisan beer. The craft brew pub will offer other Missouri beers in bottles as well as his own Yadkin, named for the waterway that runs near the building, on tap.

Missouri Hick Bar-B-Q
913 E. Washington
Cuba, MO 65453

112 E. Main
Steelville, MO 65565

www.missourihick.com
573-775-6791

Sundays - Thursdays:
11 a.m. - 9 p.m.
Fridays - Saturdays:
11 a.m. - 10 p.m.

Smoked Turkey Bake
Serves 6-8

Cooking spray
1 (10.5-ounce) can cream of chicken soup
⅓ cup milk
1 teaspoon Italian herbs of your choice
2 cups new potatoes, cut into chunks
3 cups smoked turkey, shredded
16 ounces frozen mixed vegetables, thawed
½ cup shredded cheddar cheese
1 (12-ounce) can refrigerated buttermilk biscuits, separated and cut into quarters
½ cup shredded cheddar cheese to sprinkle on top

Preheat oven to 375°F. Spray a 9x13-inch baking dish with cooking spray.

In a large bowl, stir together the cream of chicken soup, milk, and Italian seasoning until well combined, then mix in the new potatoes, shredded turkey, mixed vegetables, and ½ cup of cheddar cheese. Gently stir the cut-up biscuits into the mixture until coated, and spoon the mixture into the prepared baking dish.

Bake in the preheated oven until the top of the casserole is deep golden brown and the biscuits are no longer doughy inside, 35 to 40 minutes. Sprinkle remaining cheddar cheese on top, and return to oven; bake until cheese topping is melted, an additional 4 to 6 minutes.

ROUTE 66 FUDGE SHOP
CUBA

Caramel
Makes about a dozen pieces, depending on size

Equipment needed: 1 candy thermometer

1 cup sugar	½ cup heavy whipping cream
½ cup white corn syrup	(at room temperature)
⅛ cup water	1 teaspoon vanilla
	1 tablespoon butter

Butter an 8x8-inch or 9x9-inch nonstick pan and set aside. Put sugar, corn syrup, and water in a heavy saucepan. Bring to a boil over medium heat. Continue to boil at medium heat, stirring occasionally, until mixture starts to turn a golden brown. Remove pan from heat and slowly add the cream. (Be careful not to get burned as this will boil up, creating steam.) After all the cream is incorporated into the mixture, return pan to the heat. Stirring occasionally, cook until candy thermometer reaches 240°F.

Remove pan from heat and stir in vanilla and butter until well blended.

Pour into prepared buttered pan and allow to completely cool, about one hour.

*This caramel can be used in many recipes, such as Turtles, Chocolate Covered Caramels, added to Fudges, and whatever else you'd like to use caramel for.

Specialty Baby Cakes are dipped in dark chocolate at Route 66 Fudge Shop.

When you're in Cuba, you won't want to miss the Route 66 Fudge Shop. First of all, you'll get a warm Missouri welcome from shop owner Kelsey Schmidt, and then you'll be drawn to the confections. Kelsey learned the business from family member and original owner, Marcia Wilson, and now she's elbow deep in cocoa, making upward of 2,000 specialty Baby Cakes a week. These mini gems are made of dark chocolate pound cake dipped in rich dark chocolate. Another family member, Grace Wilson, first made them, and now Kelsey can't keep them on the shelves.

Kelsy also makes Route 66 Candy Bars, fudge, turtles, chocolate and peanut butter combinations, clusters, and more. She sells wholesale to other shops, ships chocolates on request and swears by attention to detail in her creations. Her favorite morsel? Route 66 Old Fashioned Fudge.

"Because it's sugary!" she laughs. "It's like what your grandmother used to make with cocoa and sugar."

She not only inherited family recipes but Marcia's expert advice.

"The whole secret is the right temperature," Marcia says. "You have to be patient and let fudge cool down before you add the butter and vanilla. Then stir until your arm falls off."

Kelsey buys everything locally, from the butter and eggs to the milk. Even her packaging is produced in Missouri, though not in Cuba. She bakes on Mondays and has her routine down so well that she can make three batches of Baby Cakes batter at a time. She cleans, sprays, and loads the pans on a rotation every nine minutes. Two hundred twenty cakes emerge out of a triple batch. Tuesdays are for specialty candy like the turtles plus chocolate-covered Oreos and pretzels, and Wednesday is fudge day; this pace from a woman who also owns the flower shop next door and has floral arrangements on her mind. But one conversation with her and you'll see that she's got energy to spare.

Kelsey welcomes visitors from all over almost every day: Germans, Australians, Brits—all stopping in for a bit of sweetness along Route 66 and Kelsey's friendly welcome.

Route 66 Fudge Shop
705 W. Washington Street
(Old Highway 66)
Cuba, MO 65453

Find on Facebook
ceflorist@yahoo.com
800-698-1406
573-885-1121

Mondays - Fridays:
9 a.m. - 4:30 p.m.
Saturdays:
9 a.m. - Noon

Call for extended holiday hours.

Marcia Wilson

WINDING BROOK ESTATE
EUREKA

Missouri lavender farm offers lunch and libations.

by contributor Barbara Carrow

Winding Brook Estate makes it easy to fall in love with lavender. Located in Eureka, the commercial lavender farm features 5,000 organically grown lavender plants and a bucolic setting that is an oasis for the soul.

In high season, mid-June through July, the lavender puts on its biggest show, soothing the senses with the stirring sight of endless purple blossoms, the drone of bees, and a fresh, woodsy fragrance. The blooming period slows for a while, and then, weather permitting, the plants give a repeat performance, stopping only after a hard freeze. "U-pick" lavender is generally available until October 31.

Owners Deborah and Steve Nathe were living in the fast lane, traveling all the time for their demanding sales careers on the West Coast. They longed for a change. Suddenly Deborah recalled a friend who had considered becoming a lavender farmer. "It just popped into my head," she says. Then they also recalled the acreage in Missouri that Deborah's family had bought and lived on for a short period forty years ago, when she was in high school. The 17-acre parcel was still owned by the family.

Steve was skeptical at first. But then they started researching and visiting lavender farms throughout the country. Finally, they tried planting it. The lavender flourished, and they opened the farm to visitors in July 2005.

Visitors wander among the rows of lavender and watch bees, butterflies, and hummingbirds flit from blossom to blossom as they clip bouquets. A quaint 100-year-old farmhouse hosts a gift shop where merchandise includes lavender bath and body products, lavender tea, pastries, desserts, and more.

Six times each spring and fall, Winding Brook Estate offers tea luncheons in the barn, at which lavender shows up in a variety of dishes, including lavender cream puffs or strawberries dipped in lavender-flavored chocolate.

On summer evenings, guests enjoy Lavender and Libations, with entertainment, cocktails, and appetizers, many featuring lavender as an ingredient, of course.

Natural remedy proponents claim lavender relieves stress. Steve agrees. Farming can be hard work, but he says, "I stop. I look around, breathe deep, and just take in the simple beauty of the lavender and the farm itself, and then I keep going."

Winding Brook Estate
3 Winding Brook Estate Drive
Eureka, MO 63025

www.windingbrookestate.com
636-575-5572

Early February - March 1
Thursdays - Saturdays:
10 a.m. - 3 p.m.
weather permitting

May - December
Wednesdays - Saturdays:
10 a.m. - 4 p.m.

Sundays:
Noon - 4 p.m.

Check web site for classes and special event dates.

ST. JAMES WINERY
ST. JAMES

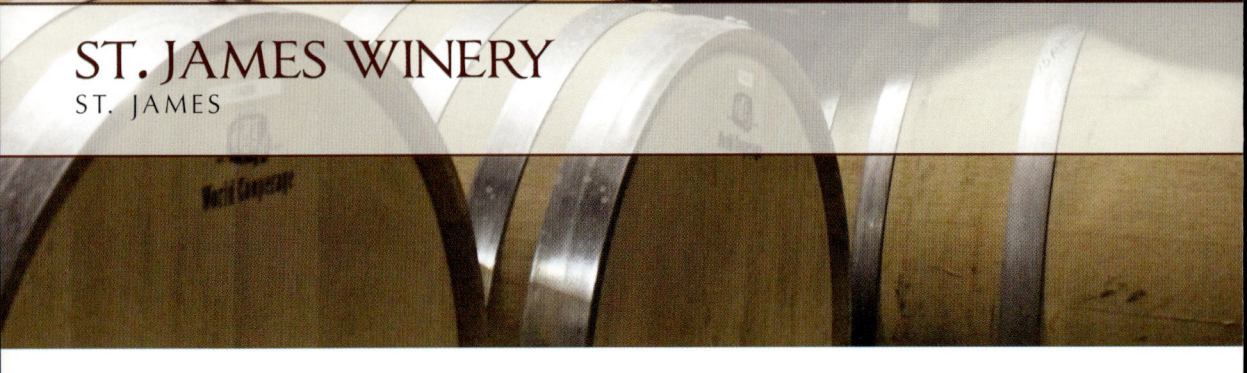

St. James Winery, Missouri's largest, owes its heritage to Italian immigrants.

The love for wine and food and the search for the great match between them is what motivates Peter Hofherr of St. James Winery in St. James. His parents, James and Pat, began the winery in 1970, producing 3,400 cases, with a wish to resurrect the area's first industry: grapes.

Though German settlers may come to mind when you think of Missouri wines, the St. James area owes its heritage to the Italian immigrants that came in the 1800s. These settlers brought with them a love of the vine, and they eventually cultivated more than 2,000 acres of vineyards before Prohibition. "Our first vineyard manager was Italian," Peter says, and his children were educated at a nearby schoolhouse, the Friendship School, now under the care of the local Veterans of Foreign Wars chapter.

This attention to community and vine has paid off: St. James Winery continues today as Missouri's largest winery, producing more than 200,000 cases per year. The growth of the winery came from careful stewardship, Peter says, and attention to the vineyard.

"Wine is an expression of the land through the grapes," he says. That focus is the challenge. "It takes a certain person to do this. Can you make a world-class wine in a region that doesn't grow *vinifera* grapes? If you like unstructured problem solving, this is a great industry."

The answer to Peter's question appears to be yes. St. James Winery has won not only the Missouri Governor's Cup several times over the years, but national and international awards as well.

Though Peter has been Director of Agriculture for the state of Missouri, a businessman, and now chief executive officer of St. James Winery, he began more humbly in the family wine business.

"I started at nine years old carrying out cases. The better jokes I had, the better tips I got."

Like his parents, he learned the business from the ground up.

St. James Winery
540 State Route B
St. James, MO 65559

www.stjameswinery.com
info@stjameswinery.com
800-280-9463

Sundays:
9 a.m. - 7 p.m.
Mondays - Saturdays:
8 a.m. - 7 p.m.

Fruit Wine Crepes
Makes about 8 large crepes

16 ounces fresh strawberries, washed and sliced
½ cup St. James Strawberry Wine
12 ounces whipping cream or topping
1 cup flour
¼ teaspoon salt
¼ teaspoon sugar
2 eggs
½ cup milk
½ cup water
2 tablespoons butter, melted

Place the sliced strawberries and the St. James Strawberry Wine in a medium bowl. Cover and refrigerate. Combine flour, salt, sugar, and eggs. Slowly add milk, water, and butter. Whisk until smooth. Preheat a nonstick skillet (or lightly oiled frying pan) over medium heat. Pour about ¼ cup batter into pan while turning pan in a circular motion to coat surface evenly. Cook until bottom is slightly brown, about 2 minutes. Loosen with a spatula and flip to the other side; cook another minute. Fold crepes in quarters so as to resemble a wedge or triangle. Place 2 crepes on a plate. Garnish with strawberry mixture and top with a dollop of whipped cream.

Note: Crepes may be made the day before serving and stored in the refrigerator. Place wax paper between crepes and cover.

SYBILL'S ST. JAMES
ST. JAMES

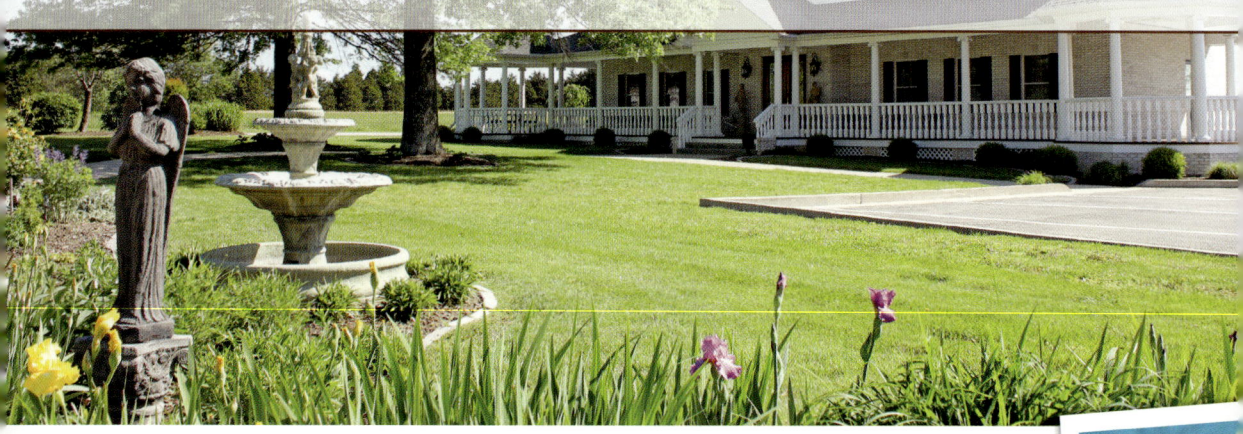

Sybill's St. James serves food made from scratch.

When Sybill Scheffer was younger, her grandparents and parents ran Zeno's in Rolla. She didn't like restaurant life then, but after trying other interests, she realized it was in her blood. With her parents, Tom and Janet Scheffer, the family opened Sybill's St. James restaurant in May 2006. The Scheffer family's history with restaurants resulted in foods made from scratch on site, and now Sybill is adding gradually to her locally sourced foods. Guests return again and again.

The restaurant is on land once known as the Dillon family farm, and the original 100-year-old farmhouse is now a gift shop run by Janet. They opened quietly, through word of mouth.

"I'd rather one person come in because of a recommendation from a friend," Sybill says, "than 10 from billboards on the highway. They come in with a different feeling, ready to expect a good experience."

Janet Scheffer, Miles Thomas Lough, Sybill Scheffer Lough, Tom Scheffer

Sybill's St. James
1100 N. Jefferson
St. James, MO 65559

www.sybills.com
info@sybills.com
Reservations recommended
573-265-4224

Sundays:
11 a.m. - 3 p.m.
Tuesdays - Saturdays:
11a.m. - 9 p.m.

Shrimp Cakes with Corn and Avocado Salsa
Serves 10-12

- 3 pounds popcorn shrimp
- 1 cup panko
- 3 tablespoons horseradish
- 1 cup celery, finely chopped
- Salt and pepper
- 1 cup mayonnaise
- 5 medium eggs
- 5 tablespoons lemon juice
- 1 cup green onion, finely chopped

For salsa:
- 1 cup corn
- ¼ cup cilantro, finely chopped
- 2 tablespoons lime juice
- ¾ cup avocado, cubed
- 3 tablespoons red onion, finely chopped
- Salt and pepper

In a food processor, pulse 2 pounds of shrimp 3 to 4 times. Do not over-process and do only 1 pound at a time. Place the processed shrimp and the remaining pound of whole shrimp together in a mixing bowl. Add the remaining ingredients and mix well. Add a little salt and pepper to taste. Form 2- to 3-inch diameter cakes about 1-inch thick. Heat a nonstick skillet over medium heat and coat with cooking spray or a little vegetable oil. Place cakes on hot skillet and cook 3 minutes per side, flipping with a spatula to cook through. For salsa, mix all ingredients together and add salt and pepper to taste.

PEACEFUL BEND VINEYARD
STEELVILLE

Peaceful Bend Vineyard was named for a three-mile bend in the Meramec.

Peaceful Bend was the old fisherman's term for the three-mile bend in the Meramec River near Steelville. Driving here, you'll meander along the waterway, as the road follows the curves of old trails. The namesake of the river bend, Peaceful Bend Vineyard, sits at the headwaters of the lazy curve, and the husband and wife proprietors, Katie Nott and Clyde Gill, make their wines down a drive flanked by tall, shady trees and older charming outbuildings. Coming along the drive, you can see this winery earns its name.

The project started for Katie and Clyde around 2000 when they bought the existing winery, built in 1972. Clyde selects grapes and creates blends pleasing to the palate. His wine list is aimed to satisfy customers' traditional tastes, some sweet, some dry, but he finds his special blends, created as his own palate dictates, sell out quickly.

Music is also a large part of life at Peaceful Bend. In fact, musicians such as the acclaimed Jacques Thibaud String Trio from Europe have performed classical music to packed wine cellar crowds. The acoustics, the backdrop of wine barrels, and the enthusiastic listeners draw visiting musicians of all genres. *Pickin' at Peaceful Bend* was recorded by national flat-picking guitar champions in 2008, and local and regional bands also play on autumn weekends. Autumn at Peaceful Bend is a lovely experience: all those trees, the music, and, well, the peace.

Huzzah Valley Wine Smoothie
Serves 4

1 cup frozen strawberries
1 cup frozen blueberries
1 cup frozen raspberries
1-½ cups Huzzah Valley Wine

Add all the ingredients into a blender and blend until smooth. Use more wine if you prefer a thinner texture to your smoothie.

Peaceful Bend Vineyard
1942 Highway T
Steelville, MO 65565

www.peacefulbend.com
winery@peacefulbend.com
573-775-3000

Sundays - Saturdays:
11 a.m. - 6 p.m.

Peaceful Bend Green Salad

Pairing: accompany this tangy salad with Forche Renault; serves 2-4

6 cups spinach
½ cup garlic-flavored feta cheese, crumbled
2 avocados, diced into large chunks
6 green onions, sliced
2 tablespoons olive oil
1 tablespoon Dijon mustard
1 teaspoon paprika
1 large clove garlic, finely minced
½ cup plain yogurt
Maple syrup or honey (optional for small drizzle)

Toss spinach, feta cheese, avocado, and green onions together in a large bowl.

Make dressing by whisking together the olive oil, mustard, paprika, and minced garlic. Stir in the yogurt. Taste and decide whether to add maple syrup or honey to taste.

Just before serving, coat the salad with the dressing.

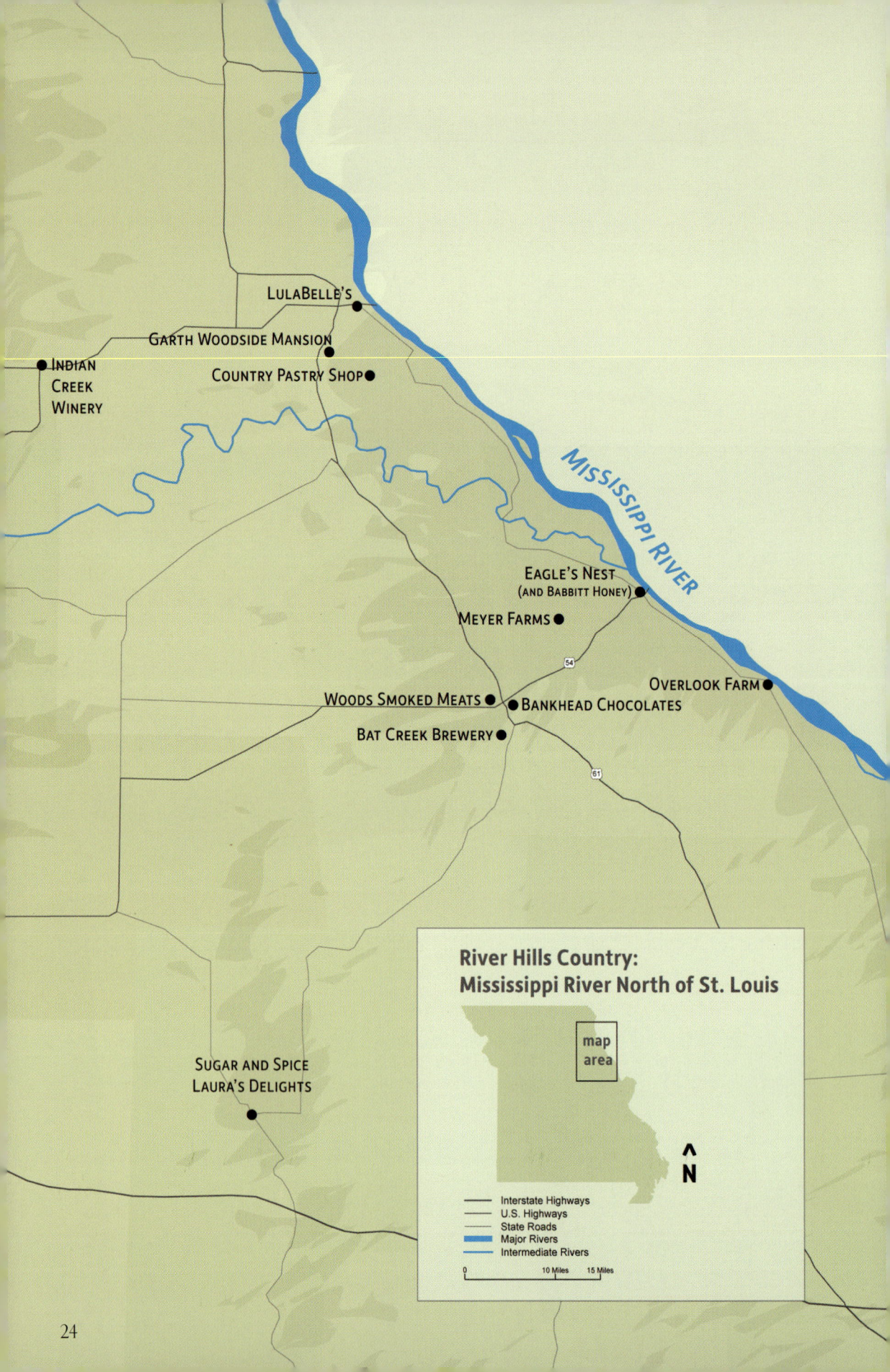

River Hills Country: Mississippi River North of St. Louis

- LulaBelle's
- Garth Woodside Mansion
- Indian Creek Winery
- Country Pastry Shop
- Eagle's Nest (and Babbitt Honey)
- Meyer Farms
- Woods Smoked Meats
- Bankhead Chocolates
- Overlook Farm
- Bat Creek Brewery
- Sugar and Spice Laura's Delights

Legend:
- Interstate Highways
- U.S. Highways
- State Roads
- Major Rivers
- Intermediate Rivers

0 — 10 Miles — 15 Miles

Mississippi River Hills
North of St. Louis

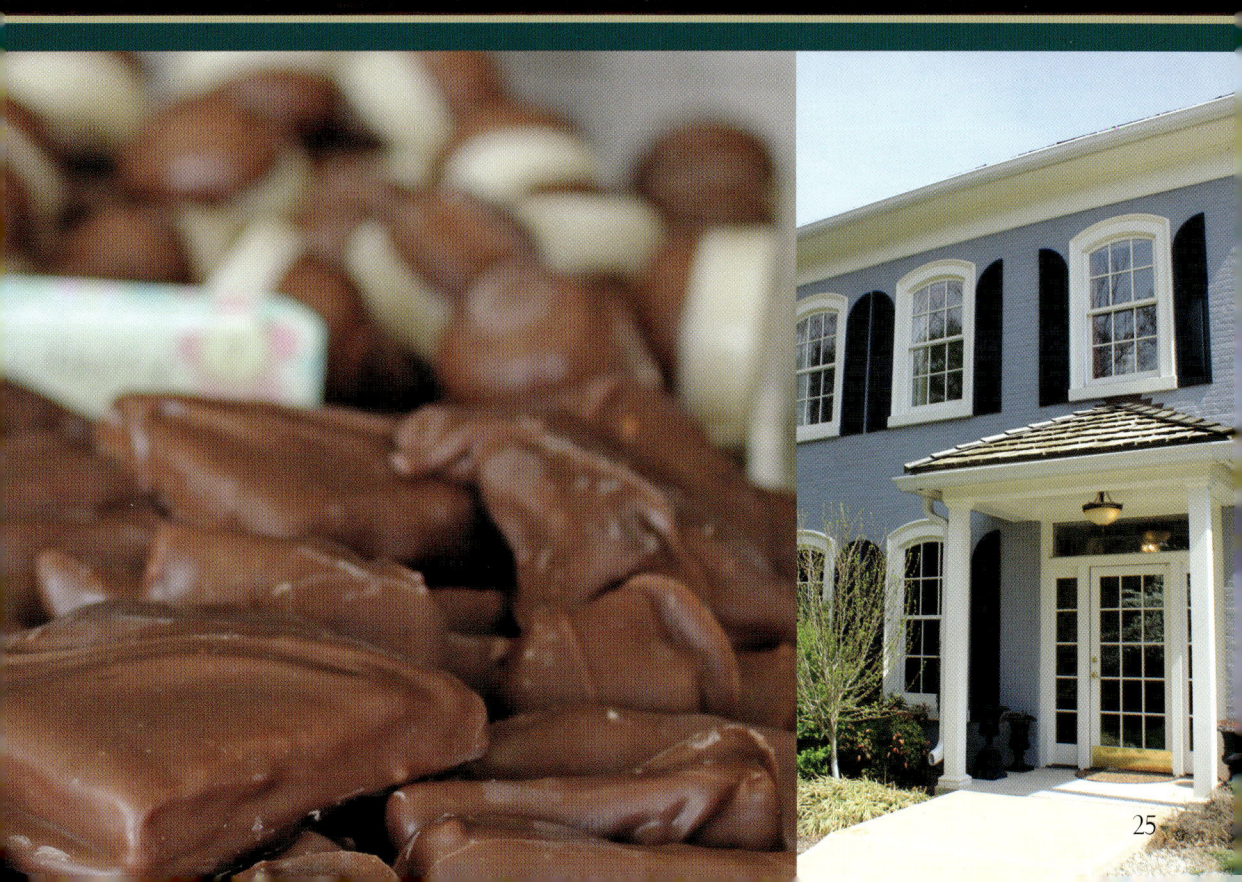

BANKHEAD CHOCOLATES
BOWLING GREEN

Customers favor old-fashioned turtles at Bankhead Chocolates.

Laura Portwood makes chocolates the old-fashioned way at Bankhead Chocolates in Bowling Green. "All the chocolates are made by hand here, in a copper kettle, with no wax in the chocolate. The ingredients are as fresh as possible," she says. This attention to detail comes from years of perfecting turtles, caramels, and bonbons, first with her mother and now with her daughter, April, who is learning candy techniques daily. Proper heat, timing, and texture are key at the shop, a pleasing, open space with candy counters and a lunchtime bistro.

"I've learned the hard way," Laura says of adjusting recipes. "Two degrees of heat can make a world of difference." That means she pays attention to the outside weather as well as the stovetop. "If it's humid outside, I adjust my temperature or risk sticky candy."

Bankhead started in 1919 with Thomas Jefferson Bankhead, a great-grandson of President Jefferson. That family, no longer in the chocolate business, left a legacy of recipes that the Portwoods now craft. Laura likes new flavor combinations, too, and experiments with ingredients such as sea salt with dark chocolate, among other favorites, tinkering with recipes until she gets it to her taste. Daughter April favors milk or even white chocolate confections. But turtles are the all-time customer favorite. In any given year, Bankhead Chocolates makes 10,000 pounds of turtles, plus 30,000 pounds of other candies. The caramel in the turtles is soft and noticeably creamy. When Laura was a child, she remembers thinking they were the "cream of the crop" and waited for chances to taste one. Customers agree. "If there are no turtles, we might as well shut the doors," Laura says with a laugh.

On a typical day, Laura gets the kettle going at about 6 to 7 a.m., and bells are dinging in the kitchen soon after as caramel reaches the temperature Laura requires. Toffee gets made and is dished out, and six to eight 55-pound batches of turtles are assembled on top of marble tables per day. Before Christmas, it's not unusual for Bankhead Chocolates to ship 100 packages of confections a day to customers throughout the surrounding area. People drive out of their way to stop here, and a taste will tell you why.

Bankhead Chocolates
810 N. Business Highway 61
Bowling Green, MO 63334

www.bankheadchocolates.com
info@bankheadchocolate.com
573-324-2312

Candy Counter
Mondays - Fridays:
9 a.m. - 5 p.m.
Saturdays:
9 am. - 3 p.m.

Bistro
Wednesdays - Fridays:
11 a.m. - 2 p.m.

Molasses Puffs
Makes about 24 pieces, depending on size

1 cup white sugar
1 cup light corn syrup
1 tablespoon white vinegar
1-½ tablespoons baking soda

Chocolate to dip:
1 pound dark or milk chocolate, melted

In a saucepan, combine sugar, corn syrup, and vinegar. Cook and stir until it reaches 300°F. Remove from heat, add baking soda. Mixture will foam up. Pour into greased 9x13-inch pan as mixture continues to rise in the pan. Candy will harden as it cools. Take out of pan when completely cool and break into chunks. Dip in chocolate.

27

BAT CREEK BREWERY
BOWLING GREEN

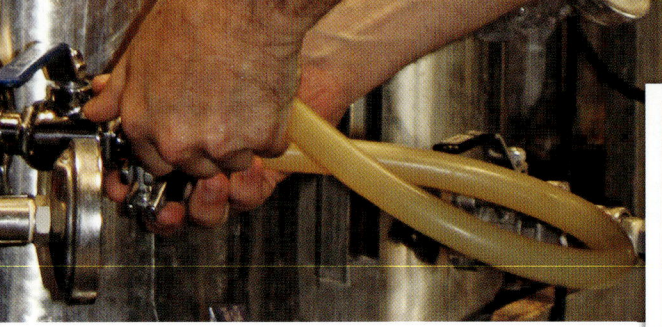

Bat Creek Brewery makes beer using wild local hops.

They were high school friends together in Bowling Green, and now they brew beer. Since 2009 the group, Jeremy Gilbert, Ryan and Heather Daffron, and more recently, Chuck Beatty, has been brewing a lot of interest in their craft beers at Bat Creek Brewery. So much so, they can't keep any in stock. So much so, they are going from a one-and-a-half barrel outfit to a 15-barrel-per-week brewery to keep up with demand.

Despite all this, there does not seem to be any frantic activity at the machine shed, the current home for the brewery. Jeremy, brewmaster, calmly talks about the beers and occasionally gets up to check a valve on a batch in process. He, Ryan, and Heather did more and more home brewing after they left college. Soon, Heather suggested they give an actual brewery a try and remove themselves from her basement. They agreed, and now they also produce a limited amount of wine: a dry oaked Norton called Platinum Reserve, a Cort Noir called Gold Reserve, and an unoaked Norton labeled Silver Reserve.

Chuck Beatty, also a high-school friend, joined Jeremy, whose business card reads Chief Brew Dude, and Ryan (Chief Beer Officer), in time to make the jump to more production. Jeremy says people are looking for a larger flavor profile than they get in mass-marketed beers. "There are hundreds of varieties of grains, hops, yeasts. I get to tailor the taste," Jeremy says. In fact, he actually found hops growing wild along a creek bed on a local Pike County farm when he was hanging a deer stand with his brother. He calls it Tepen Mystery Hop and uses it for its aroma.

Jeremy enjoys pairing craft beers with foods and hopes to highlight some locally produced foods alongside his beers in a wine and beer garden at the machine shed site.

He rises and peers over the lip of a tall stainless cylindrical vat and carefully adjusts a tap. "Not all craft beer is dark and has extreme flavor," he says as he sits again. There's something at Bat Creek for most beer drinkers.

For now, you can find Bat Creek Brewery beers in Cross Roads General Store in Bowling Green, on tap at Wings-n-Things in Hermann, and in select locations from St. Louis to Centralia and Moberly to Eolia. Look for Machine Shed Stout, Midwest Farmer's Daughter Ale, Flip Nut, Heartland Wheat, or Pike County Pale, the latter named because of those local hops. Bat Creek has seasonal brews available as well.

Bat Creek Brewery
4 W. Main
Bowling Green, MO 63334

www.batcreekbrewery.com
573-324-3258

By appointment at
the Machine Shed
in Bowling Green

Bat Creek Easy Beer Bread
Makes one loaf

3 cups self-rising flour (or use all-purpose flour plus 3-½ teaspoons baking powder and 1-½ teaspoon salt)
3 tablespoons sugar
12 ounces Midwest Farmer's Daughter Ale, warm
½ stick salted butter

Mix dry ingredients together and slowly add beer. Mix until well incorporated. Set aside for 15 to 20 minutes. Place dough in a greased and floured loaf pan. Bake at 350°F for 45 minutes. Melt butter and brush top of loaf. Return to oven for another 15 minutes. Serve with honey butter for a sweet treat that pairs well with Midwest Farmer's Daughter Ale!

Jeremy Gilbert

Machine Shed Stout Beef Stew
Serves 6 to 8

3 tablespoons canola oil
¼ cup all-purpose flour
2 pounds boneless chuck roast, trimmed and cut into 1-inch cubes
½ teaspoon salt
5 cups white onion (about 3 onions), chopped
1 tablespoon tomato paste
4 cups fat-free, lower-sodium beef broth
1 (22-ounce) bottle Bat Creek Brewery, Machine Shed Stout
½ teaspoon salt
1 tablespoon raisins
1 teaspoon caraway seeds
½ teaspoon black pepper
1-½ cups carrot, sliced diagonally ½-inch thick (about 8 ounces)
1-½ cups parsnip, sliced diagonally ½-inch thick (about 8 ounces)
1 cup turnip, peeled and cubed into ½–inch cubes (about 8 ounces)

Heat 1-½ tablespoons oil in a Dutch oven over medium-high heat. Place flour in a shallow dish. Sprinkle beef with ½ teaspoon salt; dredge beef in flour. Add half of the beef to pan; cook 5 minutes, turning to brown on all sides. Remove beef from pan with a slotted spoon. Repeat procedure with remaining 1-½ tablespoons oil and beef.

Add onion to pan; cook 5 minutes or until tender, stirring occasionally. Stir in tomato paste; cook 1 minute, stirring frequently. Stir in broth and 12 ounces of beer (savor the rest as a cooking reward), scraping pan to loosen browned bits. Return meat to pan. Stir in remaining ½ teaspoon salt, raisins, caraway seeds, and pepper; bring to a boil. Cover, reduce heat, and simmer 1 hour, stirring occasionally. Uncover and bring to a boil. Cook 50 minutes, stirring occasionally. Add carrot, parsnip, and turnip. Cover, reduce heat to low, and simmer 30 minutes, stirring occasionally. Uncover and bring to a boil; cook 10 minutes or until vegetables are tender. Serve with additional stout. Cheers!

WOODS SMOKED MEATS
BOWLING GREEN

Woods Smoked Meats has won more than 550 awards for tastiness.

The walls are lined with awards at Woods Smoked Meats in Bowling Green. Apple-maple bratwurst, beef summer sausage, buffalo summer sausage, elk summer sausage, applewood smoked bacon, smoked Canadian bacon, smoked turkey, and more have received international recognition, bringing home Gold and Silver from Germany and landing Best of Show at stiff competitions such as the 2012 Hermann Wurst Fest in Missouri. Ed Woods is one of a select group of people voted into the American Association of Meat Processors Cured Meats Hall of Fame. Ed and his wife, Regina, understate their accomplishments, but Woods Smoked Meats has received more than 550 awards.

Ed has been interested in meats since he was 12 years old when his father started the business. After getting his degree in food science and nutrition from the University of Missouri, he worked elsewhere for two years and then came back to Pike County. He settled on a brand name for the family's products, Sweet Betsy from Pike, based on the folk song. In waltz time, it declares "Oh, don't you remember sweet Betsy from Pike? She crossed the broad prairies with her husband, Ike. With a two yoke of oxen, an old yellow dog, a tall Shanghai rooster and one spotted hog." This humor and folk warmth still infuses what the Woods do in modern Pike County.

In the office, several award plaques, photos, and a map with tiny colored bits of paper attached to places Ed and Regina have visited line the walls. A bulletin board with thumbtacks holds notices, important dates, and phone numbers in place. It is clearly a place of work, utilitarian and focused on product. But those colored bits on the map are less so. "In 1995, I went to Turkmenistan for one month to help set up a sausage shop," Ed says. The trip, set up by Winrock International, sponsored two people to go. The other person turned out to be another Missourian and friend, Morris Burger of Burgers' Smokehouse in California.

"I lost 25 pounds," Ed says, but the trip got him hooked not only on service, but on travel. The couple has been to China to visit meat plants as well as to Germany and Austria to see state-of-the-art facilities. "A lot of stainless steel there," Ed says.

The taste says it for the Woods. Meats have been their focus for more than 40 years. A visit will show you the care taken with each Sweet Betsy from Pike product. Visitors and locals alike stop by at lunchtime for filling and tasty roast beef, ham, or turkey sandwiches, and there are plenty of other products to browse through in the Woods' shop.

Woods Smoked Meats
1501 Business Hwy 54 W.
Bowling Green, MO 63334

store.woodssmokedmeats.com
info@woodssmokedmeats.com
800-I-LUV-HAM
800-458-8426

Mondays - Fridays:
8 a.m. - 5:30 p.m.
Saturdays:
8 a.m. - 2p.m.

Sweet Betsy from Pike Ham Glazed with Southern Comfort
Recipe from Fern Meiser; serves 8

1 (8 to 10 pound) Sweet Betsy smoked ham
Whole cloves
1 cup Southern Comfort
¼ cup dark molasses
¼ cup brown sugar

Preheat oven to 275°F. Place ham on rack in an open roasting pan. Bake until heated throughout, allowing about 10 minutes per pound. About 40 minutes before the ham is done, score the fat in a diamond pattern with a sharp knife. Set a clove in the center of each diamond. Mix together the Southern Comfort, molasses, and sugar. Brush ham frequently with glaze during last 40 minutes of cooking.

OVERLOOK FARM
CLARKSVILLE

Historic Overlook Farm features organic and local food.

Nathalie Pettus has a lot on her plate, especially locally grown, regionally sourced produce and meats. "It's so much more than just a restaurant here," Nathalie says. Indeed, yes. There are two inns (Cedar Crest Manor, built in 1842, and Rackheath House, built in 1860), and a well-stocked shop with a great selection of cookbooks among many other items, tilapia fisheries incorporated into greenhouses, wedding venues, farm-to-table events, and an overlook of the Mississippi River that is stunning. Nathalie is looking into fresh-water prawns, apple trees (once a staple in the area), more berries, heritage red wattle hogs, growing her own feed corn, and an on-site alcohol fuel distillery, among other projects. High energy would be your first thought, meeting Nathalie.

Nathalie's ethos is organic, local, and history-centric. With the scope of her businesses, it takes a team to get the results she wants. Tom Vogt, of Clarksville, manages a lot of the daily work behind the gardens and crops. "As he likes to say, he's my boots," Nathalie says, and between Tom and others, things happen.

Nathalie's family has strong, long ties to the area. The King of Spain afforded her great-great-grandfather, Antoine Saugrain, some 35,000 acres of Missouri land. Her other great-great-grandfather, William G. Pettus, physically penned the state constitution. Her great-grandfather purchased land near Overlook Farm today, and it became the family place. "This is my Tara," Nathalie says, the place that grounds her, the place she loves, as Scarlett O'Hara did Tara.

Come to The Station Restaurant for foods from a variety of Missouri farms: from catfish and cheese to bison and produce.

Tom Vogt and Nathalie Pettus

Overlook Farm
901 S. Highway 79
Clarksville, MO 63336

www.overlookfarmmo.com
573-242-3838

The Station Restaurant
Sundays:
8 a.m. - 8 p.m.
Mondays - Thursdays:
11 a.m. - 8 p.m.
Fridays:
11 a.m. - 10 p.m.
Saturdays:
8 a.m. - 10 p.m.

Nathalie Pettus

Angela Commean

Overlook Farms Colossal Biscuits
Chef Mike Polcyn; makes 8-10 biscuits

7 cups flour
1 tablespoon baking soda
1 teaspoon kosher salt
1 tablespoon baking powder
½ cup shortening
1 cup (2 sticks) unsalted butter
4 cups (1 quart) buttermilk
Pan spray

Preheat oven to 350°F. Place 6 cups flour in bowl; add baking soda, salt, and baking powder. Mix well with fork. Add shortening, cutting in with fork. Grate cold butter on box grater into flour and use a fork to incorporate. Add buttermilk, stirring with a large spoon until just mixed.

Take remaining flour and dust table, leaving a small pile off to the side. Turn out dough and dust with flour. Knead for a couple minutes, dusting dough with flour as needed to keep from sticking. Turn dough over and form a large ball. Slightly flatten ball out to about 3 inches thick. Do not use rolling pin. Spray baking pan with pan spray. Cut out dough into rounds and place in pan making sure they are nestled up against each other. Bake for 30 to 40 minutes until done. Brush tops with butter as soon as they come out of the oven.

Serve with honey or jam.

LULABELLE'S
HANNIBAL

A former brothel, LulaBelle's is now a restaurant.

Here, ladies' undergarments are wall art. The building where LulaBelle's Restaurant serves up food used to be a brothel in earlier days. Textile enthusiasts will note fine cotton pantaloons, camisoles, fans, and more encased in glass.

LulaBelle's sits just beyond the reach of the Mississippi behind the Hannibal levee. "The river is pretty amazing," Michael Ginsberg, co-owner, says. "It's just huge how the river affected the whole nation. During the Civil War, we had to protect the river. It enabled commerce and was the reason for settling here." The river spawned business, like the original LulaBelle's, as well as others.

Today, the foods at LulaBelle's are locally sourced when available, especially produce such as asparagus, lettuce, and tomatoes in the summertime. Chef and co-owner Pam Ginsberg is a third-generation chef. Husband Michael enjoys the hospitality business. He manages the bed and breakfast he and Pam operate. The couple came to Hannibal after living in Colorado and opened LulaBelle's in 1995.

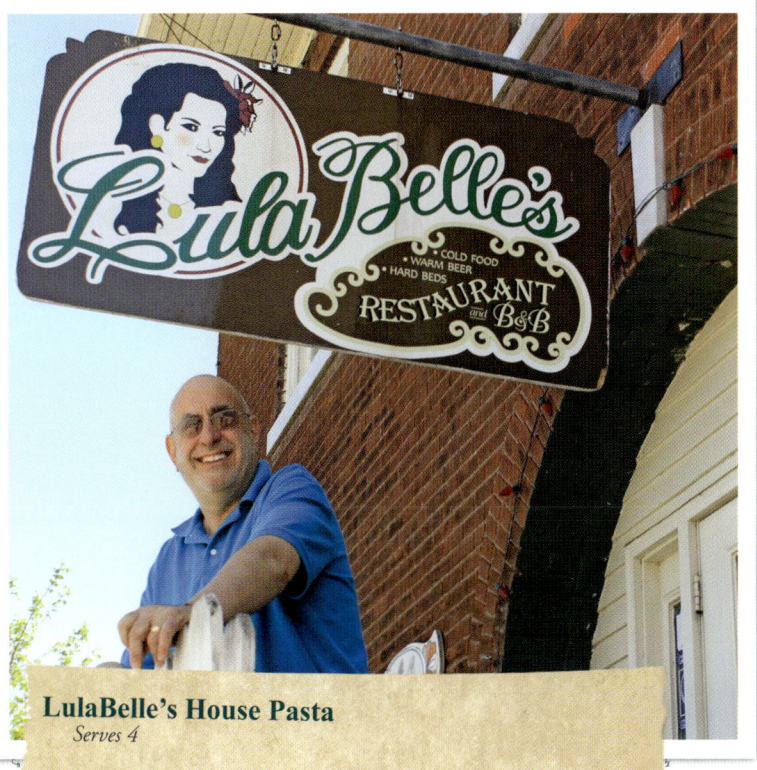

LulaBelle's Restaurant
111 Bird Street
Hannibal, MO 63401

www.lulabelles.com
573-221-6662

Lunch
Mondays - Saturdays:
11 a.m. - 2 p.m.

Dinner
Mondays - Thursdays:
4 - 8 p.m.
Fridays - Saturdays:
4 p.m. - 9 p.m.

LulaBelle's House Pasta
Serves 4

2 tablespoons olive oil
1 pound chicken breast, cut into 2-inch pieces
16 quarters fresh or canned artichoke hearts
1 cup black olives, sliced
2 tablespoons garlic, minced
2 tablespoons Italian seasoning
Salt and pepper to taste
2 tablespoons dry white wine
Alfredo sauce (recipe below)
Fettuccine noodles, cooked

For sauce:
6 tablespoons butter
2 tablespoons flour
Salt and pepper
1-½ cups heavy cream
1 cup grated Parmesan cheese
½ teaspoon nutmeg

Heat the olive oil in a saucepan over medium heat. Add chicken pieces and sauté 3 minutes or until cooked through. Add the rest of the ingredients. Sauté 2 minutes more until the garlic begins to soften. Add the white wine and Alfredo sauce. Serve over fettuccine.

Alfredo Sauce
Heat butter over medium heat. Add flour and salt and pepper to taste. Pour in cream and stir. Add cheese and nutmeg. Heat through.

COUNTRY PASTRY SHOP
HANNIBAL

At Country Pastry Shop, recipes are made from memory.

The older baking equipment came from the Pastry Box that Howard Sederwalls operated in Hannibal from 1960 to 1991. Since that time, he's put it to work outside of Hannibal at the Pastry Shop that he and Velma, his wife of 35 years, run near their home. Just about every day, they put bear claws, assorted Danish, cinnamon rolls, cream horns, dinner rolls, and butter-top or cinnamon raisin bread out on the counter. It's all made right on the spot, with both of them kneading dough lumps two at a time on a large flour-covered maple table that Howard made. The rolling pins are as long as your arm. The scoops for flour look made for giants.

Velma's been known to make pies, too, and cookies, and sage stuffing using herbs from Howard's garden for the holidays. On Saturdays...racks of breads and baked goods and go to the Colony Flea Market in Colony. They bake for three days each week to prepare. "We cut back," Velma says, but it's hard to imagine. Howard describes a specialty, macaroon cookies, reciting the recipe from memory, and you realize just how much baking wisdom the Sederwalls carry with them. Then there's their other interest: birds.

"I've cooked and baked all my life," Howard says. "I've raised birds all my life. It's just one of those things."

He raises Pharaoh Quail, a meat bird, from incubation to maturity at eight weeks. He also has Mountain Quail, Bamboo Partridge, pheasants, doves, and peacocks. The doves coo as we walk by magnificent peacocks and stunning red-gold pheasants. At one point, the Sederwalls housed nearly 40 peacocks, though now they've cut back, as they say. Howard sells his quail for $5 a piece, dressed, for a ten-ounce bird. Hobbyists can purchase Mountain Quail for $100 a pair or Bamboo Partridge for $80 a pair.

Baking and birds abound at the Sederwalls. If you stop by early, try to nab a loaf of cinnamon-raisin bread. Velma always uses three ounces of raisins in every loaf. My dreams of cream horns are dashed when I arrive at 9:30 a.m., so if you're late, you might have to be flexible and try their also-fabulous bear claw, as I did. Did I mention they've been baking all their lives? Recipes by memory? Large, floured table? Rolling pins as large as your arm?

The bear claws are good.

Country Pastry Shop
10859 Highway O
Hannibal, MO 63401

573-221-9162

Tuesdays - Fridays:
8 a.m. - 4:30 p.m.

GARTH WOODSIDE MANSION
HANNIBAL

Garth Woodside Mansion belonged to life-long friends of Mark Twain.

Along a winding drive under a canopy of large branching trees sits Garth Woodside Mansion near Hannibal. The innkeepers, John and Julie Rolsen, offer a tasting of Missouri wine on weekends, and for the nominal $10 entry fee you receive several wine samples, a private tour of the house, and a Garth Mansion wine glass as a gift. Given that Mark Twain was a life-long friend of the Garths and that John and Julie have painstakingly renovated and furnished the home to period style, you'll find many treasures. My favored reason to go, however, is to meet John and Julie, two wonderfully transplanted Missourians, and sit in their conservatory-like dining room, or the patio, or on one of the porches that clasp the house. The land slopes up to the mansion and the grounds are gorgeous. It is a world away from any bustle you might be leaving.

Then, there are the llamas. Two Appaloosa llamas, Cookie and Lexi, graze and play behind Julie's dining room. The view is flowers, white picket fence, and llama. There's a red barn nearby and flowering roses. If the kitchen door is open, poke your head in and get the treat of watching Julie at work. The stainless steel above the ovens has recipes, a handwritten one for Garth caesar dressing and a typed one for pineapple chutney, tacked to its surface. Other surfaces have instructions written directly on them. Julie is right at home, multitasking with conversation, intriguing cooking implements, and aroma. It seems effortless.

The interplay of John and Julie with guests is warm and inviting, too. John, a retired colonel in the U.S. Air Force, handles his many jobs seamlessly. He may be the one to pour your Missouri wine and share a story or two. Taste Missouri wines, talk shop, or not, but mainly, don't miss your chance to visit with these gracious hosts.

Garth Woodside Mansion
John and Julie Rolsen
11069 New London Road
Hannibal, MO 63401

www.garthmansion.com
julier@garthmansion.com
573-221-2789

Weekend Wine Tastings
Please call ahead; hours below stand as long as there isn't a wedding.
Saturdays:
11 a.m. - 3 p.m.
Sundays:
Noon - 4 p.m.
Dinners by reservation only

Julie's Breakfast Pizza
Serves 2

1 tablespoon olive oil
½ teaspoon garlic, chopped
2 cups heavy cream
Dash of nutmeg
¼ teaspoon black pepper, freshly ground
¾ cup fresh Parmesan, grated
2 naan breads (found in the Indian section of grocery stores or in Asian groceries)
Top with 2 tablespoons bacon, ¼ cup diced chicken and 2 tablespoons diced pineapple, or ¼ cup chopped spinach and ¼ cup grated Asiago cheese
4 eggs
Extra Parmesan cheese

Preheat oven to 350°F. In a saucepan, heat the oil, then sauté garlic for 1 minute. Add the cream and spices. Heat until the sauce is steaming, and then slowly add the grated cheese. Let the sauce almost boil; remove from heat and allow to cool slightly.

Pour 2 to 3 tablespoons of the sauce over each naan bread; add desired topping ingredients and fold in half. Top each naan with 2 slightly undercooked pan-fried eggs. Sprinkle with a touch of cheese and bake until bubbly about 10 to 15 minutes.

Note: Julie folds the naan and garnishes the top to serve, but you may serve flat as shown as well.

BABBITT HONEY
LOUISIANA

Seasons flavor the honey in 21 hives at Babbitt Honey.

The beehives are nestled in woods, and a faint buzzing can be heard if you step near. On closer inspection, some of the hives are hand-painted with quirky art scenes. Dennis Babbitt, beekeeper, and Martha Weston's place is a haven for the honeybee, and though the active hive dwellers don't appear to notice Dennis's artwork, what the bees produce is art itself.

Dennis began keeping bees after taking a seminar in Columbia in January 2006 and now has 21 hives that produce on average 50 to 60 pounds of honey each year. The taste is based on the surrounding nature: the woods along the Noix Creek have black locust blooming in spring; then there's clover and alfalfa in the fields; and as the season progresses, different wild flowers poke up through the underbrush and then recede. "I feel like the honey is lighter and sweeter in the spring," Dennis says. By the fall, when asters and goldenrod are blooming, the honey gets progressively darker and Dennis's palate picks out more flavor. He should know. He and Martha enjoy honey daily and put it in a lot of their cooking and baking. "It's wonderful on warm biscuits," he says.

They offer "regular" honey as well as honey flavored with lavender from Louisiana's Meyer Farm, or spices from their own herb garden, or sometimes cloves. Dennis does not heat the honey, which kills natural enzymes, but steeps it over a period of three to four months with the lavender or herbs to infuse flavors. The beehives are never treated chemically nor are the bees given antibodies that larger producers sometimes use.

For Dennis, who has owned and operated Mark Twain Hobby Center in St. Charles for 36 years, the hives appear to be his own first hobby. He spends his free time with the little fliers. "I'll take my four wheeler up there and just sit and watch them," he says. "The more you work with them, the more you realize they have an order to their house that is just phenomenal." It can be almost like therapy, he says with a chuckle. And he takes close note of all they do. "You can tell which flowers are blooming by the colors of pollen on their feet."

That rapt attention also drives the care of their land. Through controlled burning, Dennis and Martha are bringing the property back to its original oak and hickory savannah, and they see more natural grasses and undergrowth coming back each year. That's all good news for their bees, as well as anyone looking for Missouri flavor.

Babbitt Honey
can be found at:

Eagle's Nest
221 Georgia Street
Louisiana, MO 63353

Louisiana Farmers' Market
Some Saturdays:
May - October

Call Dennis Babbitt
for more information
314-401-5775

Blueberry Honey Butter
Makes ⅔ cup

½ cup fresh or thawed frozen blueberries
¼ cup honey, divided
½ cup butter, softened to room temperature

Bring blueberries and 2 tablespoons honey to boil over medium-high heat stirring constantly; cook 3 to 4 minutes or until mixture thickens and is reduced by half. Cool. Blend in remaining honey. Beat in butter. Serve spread at room temperature; store in refrigerator tightly covered.

Note: This recipe can also be used with strawberries, blackberries, and chopped peaches. It is one of Babbit Honey's bestsellers at the farmer's market.

Honey Baked Ham
National Honey Board recipe, recommended by Dennis and Martha; serves 12

Equipment needed: 1 roasting bag

1 tablespoon flour
1 (about 6 pound) bone-in fully cooked ham
16 ounces (1-¼ cups) honey
4 teaspoons lemon pepper
2 teaspoons rosemary or thyme, crushed
Honey Sauce (recipe below)

For sauce:
Ham drippings   Water   ½ cup white wine

Place flour in roasting bag and shake to coat inside surface. Place ham in floured bag. Combine honey, lemon pepper, and rosemary; pour over ham and close bag with twister. Poke holes in top of bag with fork. Roast at 325°F for 1 to 1-½ hours or until slightly browned. Remove from oven, let stand 10 minutes. Cut bag and remove ham, following bag manufacturer's directions. Reserve drippings for sauce.

Honey Sauce
Strain drippings and measure; add enough water to equal 2 cups. Add ½ cup white wine and bring to boil. Serve with ham.

41

EAGLE'S NEST
LOUISIANA

Diverse European heritage influences the food at the Eagle's Nest.

The Eagle's Nest sits on a downtown corner in Louisiana with the Mississippi River about a block away. The atmosphere inside is warm and inviting as is Karen Stoeckley, proprietor. As we talk, she calls out to customers as they come in or leave, asking after spouses who have been ill, talking with staff about wine orders, juggling quantities, and finishing paperwork for the Eagle's Nest Winery. She explains how she came from a food family, that her grandfather was a chef in Paris.

"At home there were lots of differences between my mother's Pennsylvania Dutch and my father's Eastern European backgrounds that created a love of a variety of foods."

Karen is also particularly interested in local foods and relates a vivid childhood memory of going to her grandmother's, pulling at branches full of dark, almost black, cherries, and eating until she could eat no more. "That's local," she says. Today, this translates into using honey from nearby Babbitt Honey and produce from Meyer Farms west of Louisiana. She sources her lamb, free-range chickens, and more regionally whenever she can.

"It was a huge influence (growing up) on a farm near Emelton, Pennsylvania. In eighth grade I took a friend, LizAnn, home to dinner. It dawned on me that everything on the table came from the farm. LizAnn was horrified! She didn't realize the milk came out of an actual cow."

Today, those influences translate into delicious foods that cater to a variety of customers. "We get people coming through here on motorcycles to business people from Asia," Karen says.

To create those foods, Karen draws not only on her heritage but on the classes she has had in France, Italy, and America. She travels to Provence, France, every year to teach cooking and to learn more from the locals. "This is all a huge influence on the cuisine of the Eagle's Nest."

Eagle's Nest is composed of four buildings: there's a winery, a new bakery, a shop, a bed and breakfast, as well as the bistro and fine-dining areas. Karen decorates her interiors with paintings by her husband, artist John Stoeckley, and his book, *Reflections of Missouri*, is available. In all, at Eagle's Nest there's plenty of Missouri flavor.

Eagle's Nest
221 Georgia Street
Louisiana, MO 63353

www.theeaglesnest-louisiana.com
573-754-9888

Breakfast
Sundays:
8:30 a.m. - 10:30 a.m.
Mondays - Fridays:
7 - 10:30 a.m.
Saturdays:
8 - 10:30 a.m.

Lunch
Sundays:
11 a.m. - 2:30 p.m.
Mondays - Fridays:
11 a.m. - 2 p.m.
Saturdays:
11 a.m. - 3 p.m.

Dinner
Tuesdays - Thursdays:
5 p.m. - 8 p.m.
Fridays - Saturdays:
5:30 p.m. - 8:30 p.m.

Cioppino
Serves 4

- 2 tablespoons olive oil
- 4 garlic cloves, finely diced
- 2 cod fillets, cut in 1-inch chunks
- 12 medium shrimp, peeled
- ¾ cup clams, chopped
- 6 diver scallops or other large scallops halved
- ½ cup dry white wine
- ½ cup small tomatoes, diced and seeded
- 2 tablespoons chopped fresh parsley
- ¾ cup fish stock
- 1 pound mussels, cleaned and in shell (about 15 - 18)
- Salt and pepper
- 1 tablespoon butter
- Fresh parsley

Heat oil in large skillet, add the garlic and sauté gently for 1 minute. Add cod, cook 1 minute, add shrimp, cook 1 minute, add clams and scallop, cook 1 minute and then add the white wine and bring to a quick boil for 1 minute. Add the tomatoes, parsley, and fish stock and return to a boil, then add the mussels. Cover and steam over medium heat for 2 minutes. Add salt and pepper to taste; be careful with the salt if your stock is salty. Add the butter to glaze the sauce.

Serve in big flat pasta bowls. Sprinkle lightly with a bit of the fresh parsley. Serve with grilled French or Italian bread.

MEYER FARMS
LOUISIANA

Meyer Farms provides lavender and produce to the public.

The lavender plants line up in waving rows at Meyer Farms. You'll see them first after a lovely, winding drive out from Louisiana, and then you might notice the Little Noix Creek that runs alongside the plantings. Behind the farmhouse, Peggy and Charlie Meyer also grow produce from asparagus to zucchini, as well as strawberries, red raspberries, blackberries, cantaloupe, and sunflowers in their high-tunnel greenhouse and farm fields. This year, they have 11 different varieties of tomatoes alone.

"Our customers are receptive to different types of tomatoes, especially the yellow ones that are lower in acid," Peggy says, "and they're pretty." Some tomatoes are too juicy for sandwiches, so the Meyers are sure to have a variety.

Peggy grew up on a produce farm in St. Louis County and met Charlie when she was 18 years old. "One of our activities was farming with my father on his farm. We share that same passion." It's a focus that's lasted the 40 years of their marriage, though growing large quantities and providing produce to the public and select restaurants such as Eagle's Nest in Louisiana came more recently. "I will pay someone to clean my house," Peggy says, "so I can go outside and work in the dirt."

The Meyers are comfortable folk at ease with the lavender, chickens, two beehives, and produce they care for daily. Charlie, who works off the farm as well, has always had his own garden and was even a landscaper through college.

If you can make the Saturday morning farmers' market in Louisiana, you might catch the Meyers selling bundles of fresh and dried lavender and fresh produce or, if you're early, some of Peggy's granola muffins that have more than 20 ingredients, including shredded carrots, parsnips, nuts, and more.

Meyer Farms
17819 Highway UU
Louisiana, MO 63353

Louisiana and Lake St. Lou
Farmers' Markets
Saturdays:
8 a.m. - Noon
May - October

Or, farm tours by appointment
573-754-6540

Roasted Sweet Potatoes or Butternut Squash
Charlie and Peggy Meyer; serves 2

1 squash or sweet potato
2 tablespoons olive oil
1 teaspoon salt
½ teaspoon black pepper
1 teaspoon herbs de provence
¼ teaspoon piri piri or dried hot pepper

Preheat oven to 375°F. Peel squash and cut into 1-inch cubes. Coat with olive oil and add spices. Roast for 40 minutes.

INDIAN CREEK WINERY
MONROE CITY

Indian Creek Winery uncorks history.
by contributor Rachel Kiser

When customers buy Indian Creek wine, they are buying more than a sweet white or a dry red; they are buying history.

John and the late Sheila Osbourne began Indian Creek Winery in 2005 in Monroe City, about 20 minutes west of Hannibal. It was Sheila who decided to open the winery. She already had a catering business and bakery, so she had the skill set for running her own business. She also had a background in chemistry, which meant running a winery would be a natural fit.

In March of 2010, John and Sheila purchased 30 acres of the former Robey property, a property with history to spare. The Robey Home was to become Indian Creek Winery's tasting room, and they had plans to use the barn as the winery. The large 12-room brick home belonged to W.R.P. Jackson of Moroe City in 1917, when it caught fire, which destroyed most of the home's second floor. The Jackson family rebuilt the home some time later.

But then in 1928, the Jackson estate was sold at a sherif's sale on the steps of the courthouse to John D. Robey, co-founder of a prominent lumber company. The home stayed in various Robey family hands until the Osbournes bought it.

Today, the winery has a quaint, warm tasting room with colorful rugs on wooden floors and a brick fireplace. The property is equally appealing, with a red barn, small windmill, and scenic country setting. Although Sheila passed away in 2011, her legacy lives on through the community built around the winery.

"Our winery is local to the community, and if you're looking for a winery that has its roots in the Missouri heartland, that's what we offer," says Geoffrey Preckshot, business director.

Indian Creek Winery stands apart from other wineries in its use of custom-made bottles. Though the majority of its wines are bottled in traditional longneck bottles, some bottles come in different shapes. There is a Christmas tree bottle for the holidays and a heart-shaped bottle for Valentine's Day. The Pirate's Gold wine comes in a bottle in the shape of a pirate ship.

The winery's flagship wine are a Norton, a Riesling, and four fruit wines: blackberry, strawberry, sweet cherry, and peach. In 2010, the winery won first place in the Governor's Cup for its Vignoles.

Indian Creek Winery
805 Stoddard Street
Monroe City, MO 63456

www.indiancreekwine.com
573-735-1135

Saturdays:
10 a.m. - 6 p.m.

Sundays:
Noon - 6 p.m.

Other days and times by appointment, weather permitting.

Check web site for a list of retailers.

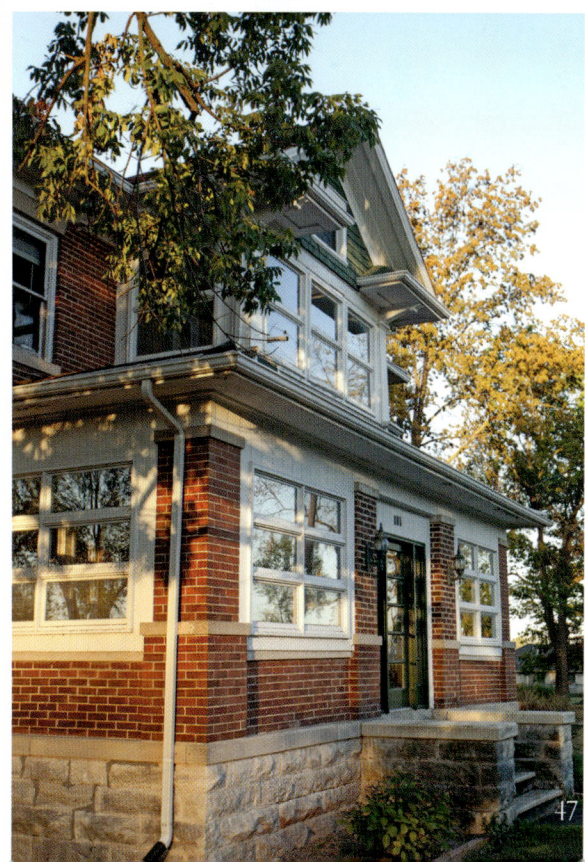

SUGAR AND SPICE LAURA'S DELIGHTS
MONTGOMERY CITY

Indulge in delicious Danish, crunchy apricot pockets, and mouth-watering pies.

If you like delicious baked goods and friendly welcomes, then Sugar and Spice Laura's Delights is the place for you in Montgomery City. Just west of the Mississippi River Hills, in the nearby flatlands, this bake shop is definitely worth a stop. Laura Gilbert makes glazed donuts that are light, apricot pockets that are crunchy and buttery with chewy, rich apricot centers, dinner rolls, buns, cookies, Danish, cream horns, coffee cakes, sheet cakes, angel food, pies, breads, and more. The list of pies alone will make your mouth water: peach, pumpkin, cherry, apple, coconut cream, blackberry, pecan, gooseberry, and mince meat. The Missouri flavors found here range through all the favorites.

When you walk in the shop, you'll notice wedding cake samples that look like hat boxes, or tiered tree trunks, or a giraffe. Red plaid curtains cover broad shelves. You'll hear the occasional sound of a train passing near by. If you peek into the back, there are icing tubes that look like gorgeous paints, a 1902 bun divider, a 15-pound rolling pin, and the wide floured surface of a work table. Laura's building has always been a bakery. Before she took up the reins in 2002, it was Joe's Pastry, and locals remember his German springerles, which Laura makes as well to continue the tradition. "I had to watch really closely while Joe made them," she says of the technique. The spongy dough, with its slightly sweet black licorice and anise taste and small pillow-like stamped squares, was a tricky recipe to learn, but the motivated Laura perfected the treat, even coming in on her days off before taking over the bakery.

"My mother says, 'I guess it's all my fault I got you that Easy Bake Oven,' " Laura laughs. She was eight or nine years old when she took over decorating family birthday cakes from her mother and has been hooked ever since. Customers walk in as we talk, and it's evident that Laura knows everyone by name. "It's senior citizens' day at the grocery store," she says, and greets a customer. A man comes in to pick up an order for his wife, and another takes two sacks home for the family. It's almost 3 p.m. and Laura has been here since before 5 a.m. She shows no fatigue, though, and the hard work seems to suit her. The treats here speak for themselves.

Sugar and Spice Laura's Delights
305 N. Sturgeon
Montgomery City, MO 63361

www.sugarnspicebakery.com
sugarnspicebakery@att.net
573-564-2573

Tuesdays - Fridays:
5:30 a.m. - 3 p.m.
Saturdays:
5:30 a.m. - 1 p.m.

Butterscotch Cookies
Makes 36 cookies

2 cups brown sugar
½ cup shortening
1-¼ teaspoons salt
3 cups cake flour
¼ teaspoon baking soda
2 large eggs
¼ teaspoon vanilla
¾ cup chopped pecans

Preheat oven to 375°F. Cream together brown sugar, shortening, and salt. Mix well, then in a separate bowl, stir together flour, baking soda, and gradually add it to the brown-sugar mixture. Mix in eggs and vanilla. Add chopped pecans. Roll dough into equal parts to make logs, refrigerate for an hour, slice off ¼-inch thick slices and bake 7 to 8 minutes.

49

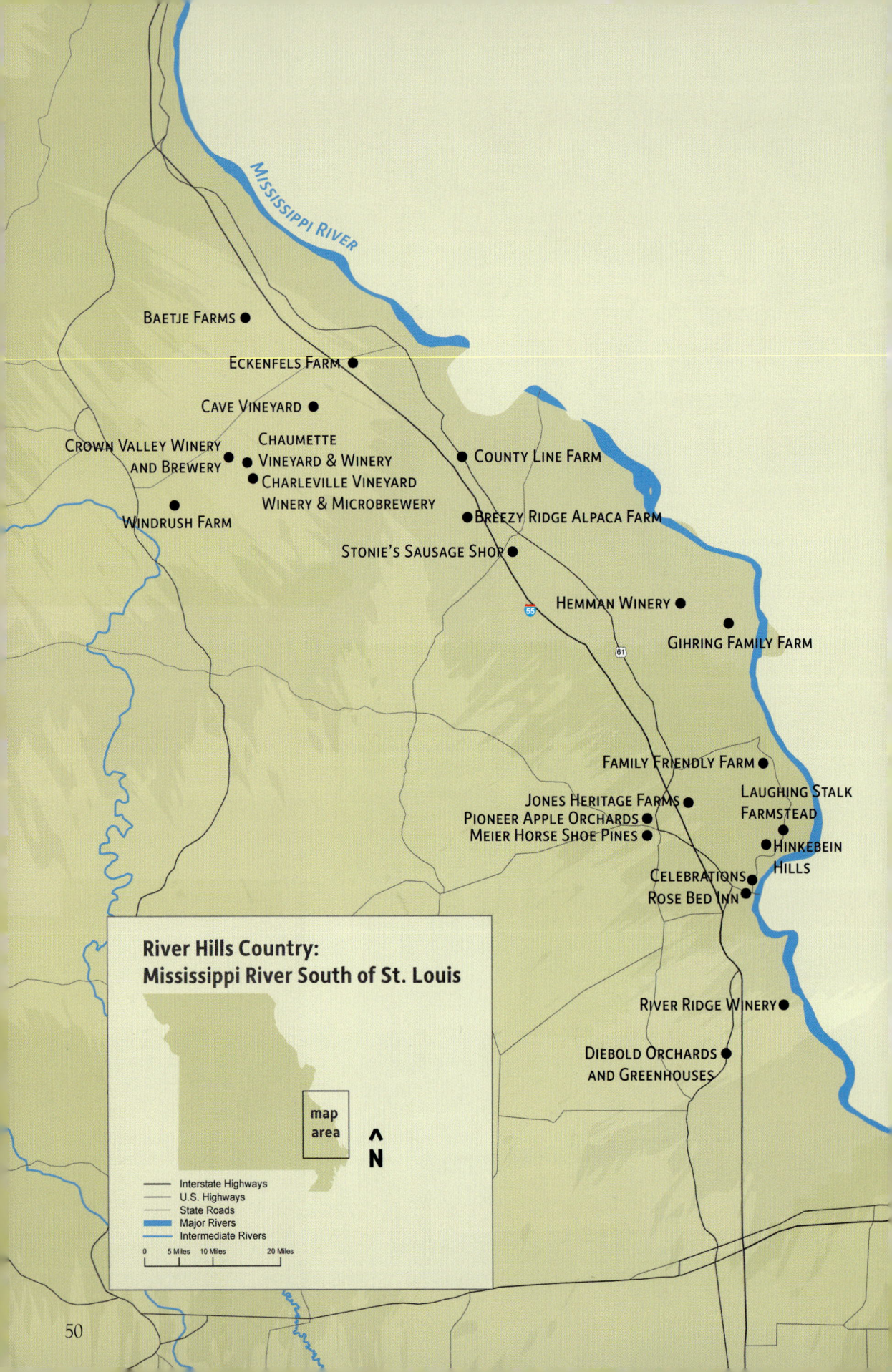

River Hills Country: Mississippi River South of St. Louis

Mississippi River

- Baetje Farms
- Eckenfels Farm
- Cave Vineyard
- Crown Valley Winery and Brewery
- Chaumette Vineyard & Winery
- Charleville Vineyard Winery & Microbrewery
- County Line Farm
- Windrush Farm
- Breezy Ridge Alpaca Farm
- Stonie's Sausage Shop
- Hemman Winery
- Gihring Family Farm
- Family Friendly Farm
- Jones Heritage Farms
- Pioneer Apple Orchards
- Meier Horse Shoe Pines
- Laughing Stalk Farmstead
- Hinkebein Hills
- Celebrations
- Rose Bed Inn
- River Ridge Winery
- Diebold Orchards and Greenhouses

map area

N

Legend:
- Interstate Highways
- U.S. Highways
- State Roads
- Major Rivers
- Intermediate Rivers

0 5 Miles 10 Miles 20 Miles

50

Mississippi River Hills
South of St. Louis

GIHRING FAMILY FARM
ALTENBURG

Real maple syrup flows at Gihring Family Farm.

When the sap is running, everyone's invited out to Gihring Family Farm in Altenburg. Warm days in January and February trigger the flow from taps that Mark Gihring sets into his 300-plus sugar maple and black maple trees growing on the farm. In an average year, the Gihrings get five or six good sap flows between mid-January and the end of February. It takes many hands to get that work complete.

Mark works into the night at times, boiling down tree sap from its natural state of 98 percent water. He watches closely so as not to over-boil his syrup, and when it hits the ideal temperature of 219 degrees Fahrenheit, he is on hand. Then filtering and canning ensues. The farm produces about 70 gallons of maple syrup, and the quart and pint jars of golden liquid sell right off the farm or, from April until October, at the Jackson and Cape Girardeau farmers' markets.

It takes about 60 gallons of sap to make a gallon of syrup, Mark says, and the process transforms mildly sweet liquid into gold. At first, Mark cooked his sap in hot iron kettles, but quickly built a cooker and what he calls the "sugar shack" for making syrup. It's worth a drive for a taste.

The Gihring's sweet life began when Christal Gihring met Mark through 4-H and small-mouth bass fishing. Mark grew up on a farm three miles from their current home, and he and Christal began making syrup in 2009. Today, their children, Jedidiah, Wyatt, Leah, and Carson, are beneficiaries of the product. "For those who haven't tried real maple syrup, there's no comparison," Christal says. "Not only is it healthier, it's just delicious."

Gihring Family Farm
856 County Road 513
Altenburg, MO 63732-9146

573-833-6384
gihringfamilyfarm@gmail.com

Call for an appointment to stop by the farm or for special orders.

From left: Jedidiah, Leah, Wyatt, and Carson

Mark and Christal Gihring

53

DIEBOLD ORCHARDS AND GREENHOUSES
BENTON

Diebold Orchards and Greenhouses sells seeds, vegetables, fruit, and fruit pies.

The Diebolds grow peaches, apples, pears, and nectarines; they also grow sweet corn, tomatoes, green beans, squash, cucumbers, and pumpkins. The family has farmed in Scott County for more than 125 years, and the farm shop and greenhouses along Highway 55 south of Cape Girardeau draw loyal locals and passers-by off the highway each season.

And it really is each season, from fruit and vegetables during the spring, summer, and fall to nut cracking and poinsettias in December. In January and February, the Diebolds begin bagging vegetable seeds for retail sale.

It all began in 1922 when Joseph Diebold planted eight acres of apples that he sold out of a garage south of Kelso. In 1945, Joseph's son and daughter-in-law planted 19 acres of peaches. By 1977, the family opened the market on I-55 and now they run year-round. This generation, it's David Diebold who is usually in the fields taking care of the orchards, and Paula Diebold primarily takes care of the market.

The Diebolds also operate a bakery at the market that features freshly baked fruit pies with fruit from their own orchard, fudge, breads, and cookies. For a busy place, there's still more planned behind the scenes: Paula would like to see the market start offering jellies of their own and apple juice for nearby wineries. They already press their own cider in the fall—another good reason to stop, sip, and shop.

Diebold Orchards and Greenhouses
217 N. Outer Road
Benton, MO 63736

pddiebold63@gmail.com
573-545-3571

Market
Mondays - Saturdays:
8 a.m. - 6 p.m.
Sundays:
11 a.m. - 6 p.m.

Diebolds' Pear Pie
Serves 8

3 cups pears, peeled, cored, and sliced
¾ cup sugar
1 teaspoon cinnamon
1 tablespoon tapioca
¼ cup coconut

Preheat oven to 350°F. In a large bowl, combine pears and sugar. Toss with the cinnamon, tapioca, and coconut. Put the pear mixture in an unbaked pie shell. Cover with another unbaked pie crust, or create a lattice top. Bake for 30 to 40 minutes or until the crust is golden.

BAETJE FARMS
BLOOMSDALE

Goat cheese at Baetje Farms wins international awards.

The gorgeous red barn is a stunner at Baetje Farms in Ste. Genevieve County. The taste of the cheeses do the rest to make you a fan. Missourians rave about these cheeses, and Steve and Veronica Baetje have won international awards as well. Their Bloomsdale was named Super Gold, one of the top 16 cheeses of the world, at the World Cheese Awards in 2011 in Birmingham, United Kingdom. It competed among 2,700 cheeses from 35 countries. The artisan cheese is a pyramid-shaped, ripened cheese seasoned with pine ash and salt.

Contrary to what the uninitiated might think, not all goat cheese tastes the same. Each farmstead cheese the Baetjes make is distinct and usually named for something close to them: Cherbourg was the street they both grew up on, Thibodeau was a French Canadian friend of the family, and Bloomsdale is the name of the nearby town.

The goats are milked twice a day, and each one delivers about one gallon. Steve is up between 1 and 2:30 a.m. on market days doing chores, loading cheese, and making deliveries on days when there is an evening market. On Saturdays, when the Baetjes and several employees run three markets, they finish work between 7 and 8:30 p.m. "You have to love it," Steve says.

Veronica started it all in 1998 when she brought home one goat because she didn't need as much milk as a cow would give. She then trained at the Vermont Institute of Artisan Cheese and took classes for milk processors and cheese makers in Wisconsin. The couple bought their farm in 2005, finding that its 1912 Sears and Roebuck kit barn was hard to resist. Now their life of cheese is in full swing. The couple started out thinking Veronica would milk 20 goats and Steve would work off the farm. Now they both work full time on the farm, and business is expanding. They milk about 50 goats and produce between 250 and 400 pounds of cheese a week from their own goats and another 250 pounds per week of sheep's milk cheese, depending on the season. "Since we make them," Veronica says, "I feel there's something special about each one. Fleur de la Vallee is smooth and velvety on the tongue. It's a challenge to make, and I like challenges." Any of the Baetje farmstead artisan cheeses are a treat. It's a Missouri taste you won't want to miss.

Baetje Farms
8932 Jackson School Road
Bloomsdale, MO 63627

www.baetjefarms.com
awardwinningcheese@baetjefarms.com
573-483-9021

Visit these farmers' markets or call or email for information.

Soulard Market, Booth 18
Fridays:
8 a.m. - 1 p.m.
Saturdays:
7 a.m. - 1 p.m.

Clayton Farmers' Market
Saturdays:
8:30 a.m. - 12:30 p.m.

Maplewood Farmers' Market
Wednesdays:
4 p.m. - 7 p.m.

Webster Grove Market
Thursdays:
3 p.m. - 7 p.m.

Tower Grove Market
Saturdays:
8 a.m. - Noon

Washington University Market
Thursdays:
10 a.m. - 2 p.m.

Goat Cheese and Caramelized Onion Pizza

This pizza has a very thin crust that may be made a few hours ahead of time. It will always be crispier when cooked on a pizza slab but may be cooked on the oven racks also. A store-bought crust may also be used.

For crust:
1-¼ cups flour
1 packet dry yeast
¾ cup warm water
1-½ tablespoon olive oil
1 teaspoon salt

For topping:
¼ cup olive oil
1 large red onion
¼ cup brown sugar
¼ cup balsamic vinegar
¼ cup red wine
½ pound spinach
Small can sliced black olives
1 package Baetje Farms Goat Cheese (best with either plain, three-pepper, or garlic and chives cheese)

Pizza Crust
In a mixing bowl combine 1-¼ cups flour and 1 packet of dry yeast. Using the dough hook attachment, blend together with ¾ cup warm water, 1-½ tablespoon olive oil, and 1 teaspoon salt. Mix at medium speed for 3 minutes, or until the dough comes away from the sides of the bowl. Knead the dough on a floured surface until smooth. Place in a greased bowl and cover. Leave for 1 hour in a warm place until the dough doubles in size. Punch down and leave 10 minutes. Roll out the dough to 12-inch diameter, prick and cook at 400°F for 15 minutes.

Topping
Heat olive oil in a pan and add sliced onion. Cook for about 10 minutes until the onion is soft. Add the brown sugar, balsamic vinegar, and red wine. Simmer for 20 minutes until syrupy. Spread onion mixture on cooked pizza crust, top with spinach, olives, and crumbled Baetje Farms Goat Cheesa. Bake at 400°F for 10 minutes.

HEMMAN WINERY
BRAZEAU

Hemman Winery makes unusual rhubarb, pumpkin, and cushaw wines.

As far as country storefronts go, Hemman Winery is a charmer. Despite a second story that was destroyed at some point in its history, the approach is sweetly nostalgic. The front porch boasts gently rocking chairs, wide-paned glass windows, and a seasonal porch special. The sunny end of the porch has a bountiful flowering vine blocking direct rays. The road in front of Hemman's curves through Brazeau, a vision of old-town America calmly situated on a Mississippi River Scenic Drive. The settlers here were Scotch Irish and they established themselves in 1819, a full 20 years before the area's more numerous German settlers. There is a Brazeau School Museum operated by the Brazeau Historical Society, and a teahouse occasionally serves as a bed-but-no-breakfast place.

Dorothy and her husband, Al, purchased the country store building in 1959 but eventually closed it as a store in 1971. Al used the building for a barbershop and work area. Then, the family began making wines on the front porch. Al had made wines since he was a teen with his mother, who had learned from her German father who immigrated in the 1840s. Soon, more formal grape pressing and bottling facilities followed, and by 2003, the Hemman Winery was established.

Today, there's a covered patio for weekend live music and planned events such as an Old Fashioned Christmas Walk with 250 luminaries, and Lucy Days, a grape stomping rout named for Lucille Ball. Inside, the winery retains the country store feeling, now with wine bottles lining the old store shelves. A wood burning stove still reigns in the middle of the floor space, and fireside specials are on offer in the colder months.

The most popular wines at Hemman are sweet with some unusual twists. Dorothy saw rhubarb wine in Iowa Amish country once, and now it's offered at Hemman. In season, pumpkin and cushaw (squash) wine are made. Blackberry wine is a favorite. The winery continues to grow each season and currently makes 2,000-plus gallons or more than 10,000 bottles per year. The family worked together to plant the 450 vines, but Al has passed on. Now Doug Hemman and his wife, Bonnie, work alongside Dorothy, continuing the tradition.

From left: Bonnie, Doug, and Dorothy Hemman

Hemman Winery
13022 Highway C
Brazeau, MO 63737

www.hemmanwinery.com
573-824-6040

Fridays:
from June 1 to December 31
1 p.m. - 6 p.m.
Saturdays and Sundays:
Noon - 6 p.m. Year-round

Blackberry Wine Cake
Serves 12

½ cup chopped pecans
White cake mix
4 eggs
3 ounces blackberry gelatin package mix (may substitute raspberry)

½ cup oil
1 cup Hemman Winery Blackberry Wine

For glaze:
1 cup powdered sugar
½ cup butter

½ cup Hemman Blackberry Wine

Preheat oven to 375°F degrees. Grease and flour Bundt pan. Put nuts in bottom of pan. Mix cake mix, eggs, gelatin package mix, oil, and wine. Pour batter over nuts and bake 50 to 60 minutes. While cake is baking, combine powdered sugar, butter, and wine in a saucepan and bring to a boil. Pour ½ of glaze over warm cake. Wait 30 minutes and pour the remaining glaze over the cake.

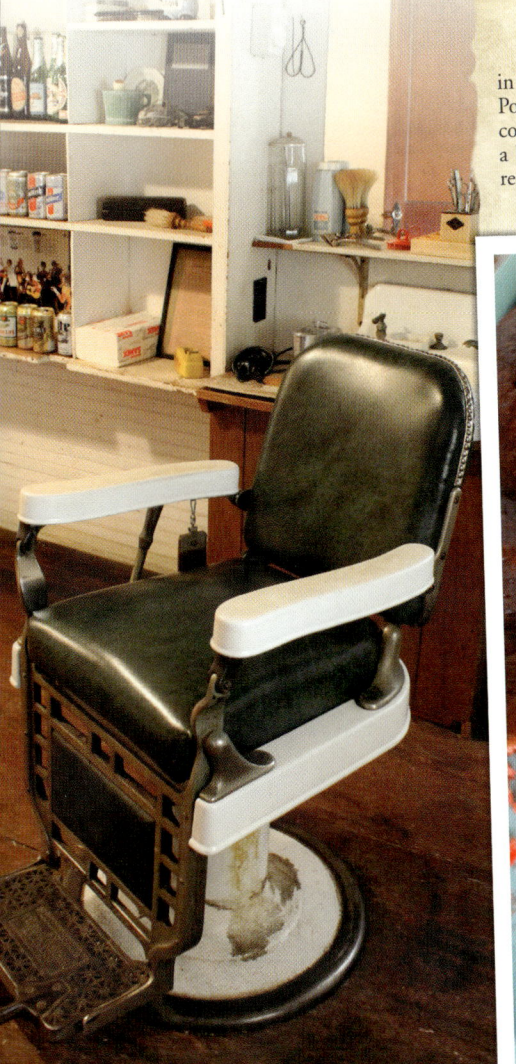

CELEBRATIONS
CAPE GIRARDEAU

Celebrations restaurant changes menu to showcase seasons.

Celebrations restaurant in Cape Girardeau has been constantly evolving since it opened in 1997. Owners James and Pat Allen were foodies and wine admirers, and when they retired, they decided to create a spot in southeastern Missouri for enthusiasts of both. Pat started catering in 1992, and their restaurant grew from there.

The menu changes often to showcase the seasons. Executive Chef DeWayne Schaaf shares the Allens' vision and sources foods as locally as possible; pork from Hinkebein Hills and Jones Heritage Farms, lamb from Ritter Hills, produce from Laughing Stalk Farmstead, and more. The foods at Celebrations create a flavor sensation on the tongue. "The beauty of this area is that we have four real seasons. The downside of this area is that we have four real seasons," DeWayne says. The menu highlights the best of each of them.

James, too, sees that the wines are top notch. In fact, Celebrations' wine list has won the *Wine Spectator* Best Award of Excellence and joins an elite group of restaurants so designated. The bar stocks Missouri beers from Charleville in Ste. Genevieve, Augusta Brewing Co., and more.

The ambience at Celebrations is relaxed, and the service is smooth. Several diners are there for special events, but you get the notion that many are regulars out for the weekend. The Allens and Schaaf offer food and wine pairings, wine dinners, and cheese flights among the menu choices. The pasta is house-made. Specialties sometimes include antelope, venison, duck, and almost always seafood.

Lemon Scented Blue Gill
Chef DeWayne Schaaf; serves 2-4

¼ cup olive oil, divided
2 (1-pound) blue gill fillets trimmed and boned (or use other light flaky white fish with small fillets, trimmed)
3 tablespoons parsley, coarsely chopped
3 sprigs of thyme
3 lemons, sliced into rounds ¼ inch thick
2 tablespoons lemon juice
1 teaspoon salt

Prepare outdoor grill and cook over medium high heat or bake at 375°F.

On the backside of a cookie sheet make an 18-inch long trough with aluminum foil by folding up the sides 2 inches and the ends 1 inch. Lightly rub the foil with a touch of the olive oil. Place the fillets on the oiled foil, then top with the parsley, thyme, and lemons. Mix the lemon juice and remaining olive oil. Pour the lemon and oil mixture around the sides of the fish. Season the fish with salt. Take another piece of foil and make a top, folding the sides together with the bottom foil, creating a pouch for the fish. Slide pouch off the cookie sheet and onto the grill or into the oven. The fish will take around 15 minutes to cook through on the grill and about 12 minutes in the oven. When fish is fully cooked, slide the cookie sheet under the pouch, lifting lightly with tongs if needed. Allow to rest for around 7 minutes before serving.

Tomato and Herb Orzo
Chef DeWayne Schaaf

3 heirloom tomatoes, cut into 1-inch cubes
1 (1-pound) box of orzo, cooked and cooled
1 tablespoon mint, finely chopped
3 tablespoons parsley, coarsely chopped
2 green onions, coarsely chopped
2 tablespoons extra virgin olive oil
2 tablespons lemon juice
2 tablespoons orange juice
Salt to taste

Mix all ingredients and allow to marinate for 2 hours or more. Allow to rest at room temperature for 1 hour before serving.

Celebrations
615 Bellevue
Cape Girardeau, MO 63702

www.celebrations-restaurant.com
celebrations615@sbcglobal.net
573-334-8330

Reservations recommended
Tuesdays - Thursdays:
5 p.m. - 9 p.m.
Fridays - Saturday:
5 p.m. - 10 p.m.

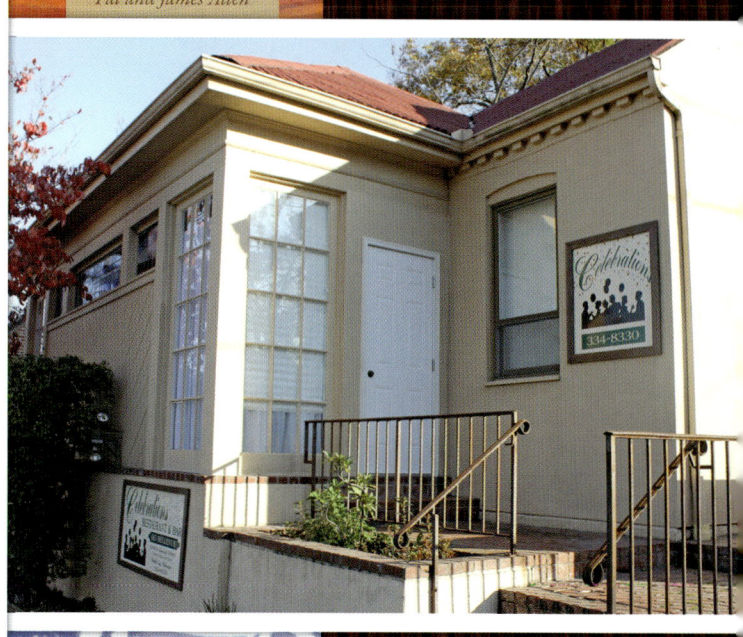

Pat and James Allen

Chef DeWayne Schaaf

Grilled Okra
Chef DeWayne Schaaf

Okra   *Optional:*
Olive oil   Minced jalapeno
Salt and pepper   Lemon juice

Lightly rub okra with olive oil. Sprinkle with salt and pepper. Grill okra on each side for around 3 minutes, or until they are tender. Serve immediately. Lemon juice and minced jalapeno are a great topping, though the okra are great on their own.

FAMILY FRIENDLY FARM
CAPE GIRARDEAU

Family Friendly Farm really is and sells chicken, eggs, milk, and more.

It's a busy life at Family Friendly Farm near Cape Girardeau. Matthew and Rachel Fasnacht started out with 100 chickens in 2004. Today, the couple and their 8-year-old son Darrell shepherd about 2,000 meat birds a year, 1,100 laying chickens, and 20 adult Jersey cows for their daily milk. Matthew, who is also a professor of chemistry at Southeast Missouri State University, believes in growing in small increments, not taking on debt, and raising animals in ethical and natural conditions. Rachel echoes that sentiment in the products she offers at their on-site farm store.

The conditions at Family Friendly Farm are gentle on animals and the people who shop there. "We're grass farmers," Matthew says. The cattle graze on annual rye grasses, sorghum-sudan grass, and fescue in rotating pastures so the soils rest and improve with the cycle. This intensive grazing system produces 15 gallons of milk a day that the Fasnachts sell in half-gallon glass containers, the necks of the jars thick with cream.

Customers mentioned their many stops along a route of local producers to find the vegetables, fruits, and other goods they wanted for the week. The trek, they told Rachel, sometimes took almost a full day to complete, and so an idea was born: Rachel made her farm shop a one-stop shop by including other farmers' goods on the shelves. The farm store, the bottom floor of the Fasnachts' two-story white farmhouse, displays a wealth of local products. In addition to Family Friendly's own chicken, eggs, and milk, customers can find local raw honey, apple butter, grass-fed beef, vegetables in season, and even Missouri-grown organic rice and popcorn from the McKaskle Family Farm in Braggadocio.

Family Friendly Farm
834 State Highway V
Cape Girardeau, MO 63701

www.familyfriendlyfarm.com
info@familyfriendlyfarm.com
573-382-3844

Farm Shop
Tuesdays:
3 p.m. - 6 p.m.
Saturdays:
9 a.m. - 3 p.m.

Garlic Lime Chicken
Serves 6

- 1 teaspoon salt
- 1 teaspoon pepper
- ¼ teaspoon cayenne pepper
- ¼ teaspoon paprika
- 1 teaspoon garlic powder
- ½ teaspoon onion powder
- ½ teaspoon thyme
- 2 tablespoons butter from grass-fed cows
- 2 tablespoons olive oil (options: use schmaltz, lard, or tallow)
- 6 pieces pastured chicken
- ½ cup chicken broth
- 4 tablespoons lime juice

In a bowl, mix together first 7 ingredients. Sprinkle mixture on both sides of chicken pieces.

In a skillet, heat butter and olive oil together over medium high heat. Sauté chicken until golden brown on each side, about 5 minutes on either side or until no longer pink in the center. Remove chicken and add chicken broth and lime juice to the pan, whisking up the browned bits off the bottom of the pan. Keep cooking until sauce has reduced slightly. Add chicken back to the pan to thoroughly coat and serve.

HINKEBEIN HILLS
CAPE GIRARDEAU

Hinkebein Hills Farm raises antibiotic- and hormone-free pork and beef.

A white, utilitarian butcher shop sits at the end of a long driveway flanked by pasture and farm equipment at Hinkebein Hills Farm near Cape Girardeau. Everything inside is handmade. On 37 acres, Karlios Hinkebein raises antibiotic- and hormone-free pork and beef. He was raised with home butchering and decided in 2007 to build his own processing plant. Today, he processes 400 hogs a year and about 50 beef cows to make brats and smoked meats for individual visitors as well as nearly 14 restaurants in St. Louis.

Karlios has also started a new venture: a food truck he takes to the Cape Girardeau Saturday farmers' market and to area parking lots. "It gives people a sampling of what our meats taste like," Karlios says. He's been stocking bulk meats like pulled pork, breakfast meats, ribs, and brisket in the truck but changes over to lunch sandwiches from 11 a.m. to 1 p.m.

Karlios credits his family—one brother, three sisters and their spouses, a niece, and other family—for the success of the farm. Judging by the locals that stop by the farm and the ones buying sandwiches along the roadside, the quality of Hinkebein Hills' meats continues to be a hit.

Hinkebein Hills Farm
434 Whispering Wind Lane
Cape Girardeau, MO 63701

hinkebeinhillsfarm@wildblue.net
573-332-8530

Mondays - Fridays:
8 a.m. - 5 p.m.
Saturday:
8 a.m. - Noon

LAUGHING STALK FARMSTEAD
CAPE GIRARDEAU

Laughing Stalk Farmstead offers organic produce to subscribers.

Gusto, a young Great Pyrenees and Newfoundland mix, greets you as his name implies, and then bounds off to help Emily Scifers and Ross Peterson by checking the perimeter of their well-tended small organic farm. It's an open, sunny slope, but he takes his job seriously, sniffing out possible canine threats. The couple moved back to Missouri after organic farming in Wisconsin and Minnesota for several years. Their farmstead near Cape Girardeau has a small greenhouse and several wheelbarrows to tend to the 40 different varieties of vegetables, herbs, and beans they grow. It takes a great deal of handwork—hauling compost by the wheelbarrow, turning it into the soil row-by-row—but the couple is motivated by the upswing of interest in organic food in Missouri.

"People are learning more about eating organically here," Emily says. "It feels great being part of the beginning movement." The couple's Community Supported Agriculture (CSA) list of subscribers is increasing. Emily hopes to expand their cultivated land to be able to have even more vegetables in the boxes for their customers. For the first time, she says, "We had a waiting list of CSA customers this year."

The couple came into farming through gardening. Ross, while teaching environmental science in a residential treatment facility in Oregon, set up a garden for his 13- to 17-year-old students. "The cook would use some of the food we grew in the meals." The project had him hooked. Laughing Stalk Farmstead, he says, feels like large-scale gardening. "Sometimes I feel like this was a leap," Emily says, and they both smile, pleased.

Laughing Stalk Farmstead
1521 County Road 649
Cape Girardeau, MO 63701

www.laughingstalk.com
laughingstalkfarmstead@gmail.com
573-576-0730

By appointment, call or email

Cape Girardeau
Farmers' Market
Thursdays:
April - Thanksgiving
2 p.m. - 6:30 p.m.

Cape Riverfront Market
May - October
Saturdays:
8 a.m. - Noon

CSA subscriptions available

Sweet Potato and Black Bean Bake
Serves 4-6

3-4 large sweet potatoes
2 tablespoons vegetable oil, divided
1 clove garlic
1 bunch (about 1 cup) scallions, chopped
1 bunch (about 4 cups) kale (or your favorite green), stemmed and chopped
4 cups cooked black beans
12 (6-inch) corn tortillas or 6 (10-inch) flour tortillas
2 cups cheddar cheese (or other of your choice), divided
12 ounces salsa

Preheat oven to 375°F. Chop the sweet potatoes into bite-size pieces and boil until tender. Drain and set aside. In a large frying pan, heat 1-½ tablespoons of the oil and add the garlic and scallions. Sauté for 2 minutes. Add the kale and sauté for another 2 to 3 minutes. Mix in the black beans and set aside when greens are coated. Use the remaining oil to grease a 9x13-inch pan. Layer like you would a lasagna, starting with the tortillas, then the sweet potatoes, then the greens and black bean mixture, using roughly half for the first layers. Top these first layers with ½ cup cheese. Repeat the second layers. Top the greens and black bean layer with salsa and finish with 1-½ cups of cheese. Bake for approximately 35 to 40 minutes or until the cheese browns.

ROSE BED INN
CAPE GIRARDEAU

James Coley

Restored and renovated Rose Bed Inn serves special meals.

The Rose Bed Inn is a turn-of-the-century house renovated and opened as a bed and breakfast by Chef James Coley and Eldon Nattier in 2001. The owners serve special meals here, by prior arrangement for small and large groups, and use fresh ingredients, local whenever possible. The welcome is warm.

The story of the Rose Bed building itself is noteworthy: condemned and boarded up, Eldon tackled the renovation of the three-story brick home and saved much of the original woodwork and structure. It was his 69th renovation project, and today the interior reflects the period of the house with added personal touches of the proprietors. Outside, too, the house reflects its owners' interests: a lovely garden complete with goldfish ponds, rose arbors, azaleas, and more surround the building. James spends his quiet moments here, and it is a pleasure to walk through. Across the road from Rose Bed is the river bridge to Illinois, opened in 2003, and a vista of the Mississippi River. It's a good setting for a meal, inside and out.

Also in the block of buildings is the recently opened Rose Water Spa that offers hair styling, facials, pedicures, manicures, and massages as well as the Aartful Rose, an art space for receptions and art viewings by appointment. The first Friday of each month there is a reception from 5 to 8 p.m. in conjunction with art events around Cape Girardeau, offering a great combination of food and art for visitors.

Rose Bed Inn
611 S. Sprigg Street
Cape Girardeau, MO 63703

www.rosebedinn.com
573-332-7673

Dinner:
By prior arrangement
Call for reservations

Eldon Nattier (left) and James Coley (right)

Basil Chicken Wellington
Serves 6

1 cup (2 sticks) butter, divided
1 tablespoon olive oil
1 cup white wine, divided
2 medium onions, diced
1 bulb garlic, crushed, divided
2 cans (3-½ ounces each) sliced mushrooms
2 teaspoons diced fresh basil, divided
6 ounces Swiss cheese, shredded
6 chicken breasts, boneless and skinless
10x15-inch sheet of puff pastry
2 eggs, beaten
2 tablespoons honey
½ teaspoon salt
½ teaspoon ground white pepper
½ cup heavy cream

Melt together 1 stick butter, olive oil, and ¼ cup of the wine. Add the onions and half the garlic, and sauté until onions are translucent. Drain mushrooms and add along with 1 teaspoon of the basil, and sauté another 5 minutes. Drain liquid and chill mixture. Once chilled, stir in cheese and set aside. Trim chicken breasts and pound between sheets of plastic wrap until uniform thickness of about ½-inch. Place a 2-ounce scoop of the mushroom and cheese mixture in the middle of each breast and gather edges over to form a ball. Place breasts in cups or large muffin tins and freeze just until they hold their shape. Cut puff pastry into 5-inch squares and roll out a bit to increase size. Cover each breast with pastry using beaten egg to seal all edges. Bake at 350°F on lightly greased baking sheet for 1 hour. While chicken bakes, sauté remaining garlic in remaining 1 stick butter until golden. Add remaining ¾ cup wine, honey, salt, and pepper. Simmer until alcohol boils off. Add cream, bring to a boil, lower heat, and simmer until reduced by one-third. To serve, ladle sauce onto plate, place chicken in center, and garnish with remaining fresh basil.

RIVER RIDGE WINERY
COMMERCE

River Ridge Winery grows French grapes on a sunny hilltop near the Mississippi River.

Jerry and Joannie Smith run a winery, the Christmas Tree and Yule Log Cabin, and the Little Log Cabin for overnight guests near tiny Commerce in the hills rolling back from the Mississippi River. It's a beautiful spot. You pass near the river on the way, and depending on the season, you'll spy wildflowers between you and the water. The country road climbs just after Commerce, and at a bend under large old oak and sycamore trees, you'll see River Ridge Winery. There is a tiered patio, a pavilion for live music and gatherings, and the refurbished white farmhouse turned into a winery shop with its welcoming attached Fermentation Room Cafe.

River Ridge wines emerge from hand-tended vineyards within miles of the winery. On a specially chosen sunny hilltop near his home, Jerry has even been able to grow *vinifera* grapes such as Cabernet Sauvignon, Cabernet Franc, Merlot, Syrah, and Chardonnay, a surprise in Missouri. The sunny slope that he devotes to these grapes has been carefully selected. He explains how even a few feet down the hill the French grape varieties will not do as well. The shadowed, slightly less elevated land where fog rolls makes production of those varieties impossible. He explains that Native Americans, French and other explorers, and trappers had long used this ridgetop, called Crowley's Ridge and which runs roughly parallel to the Mississippi, to traverse the region. The elevation of the ridge raises it above the frost line and makes it ideal for *vinifera*. His home faces a sun-washed vineyard and backs into deep woods with the rushing river below. This is a man who knows how to place things on his land.

And he loves it. Talking with Jerry, you will no doubt hear his joke of the day, but you'll also get a sense he enjoys the planning and the purpose behind all the labor. Jerry began planting grapes in 1980, after leaving the Navy as a Lieutenant Naval Aviator in 1976. Joannie began the Christmas Tree and Yule Log Cabin, just four miles away, the same year. They met and married in 1993, refurbished the century old farmhouse on Jerry's land, and opened the winery in 1994.

River Ridge has grown to producing about 7,000 gallons of wine per year. Eighty percent is sold at the winery and includes wines from grape varieties such as Vignoles, Chambourcin, Cynthiana, and Traminette. The wine names—Lucky Dog, Nooner, Ten Spot, among others less colorful—fit the fun and relaxed yet purposeful style of the Smiths. Come see for yourself.

River Ridge Winery
850 County Road 321
Commerce, MO 63742

www.riverridgewinery.com
info@riverridgewinery.com
573-264-3712 or
573-264-2747

Winery
Daily (except Christmas):
10 a.m. - 6 p.m.
Fridays:
Open until 9 p.m.

Fermentation Room Cafe
Daily (except Christmas):
11 a.m. - 6 p.m.
Fridays:
Open until 8 p.m.

Cynthiana Sauce

¼ cup olive oil
3 cups onion, chopped
3 cups mushrooms, chopped
10 garlic cloves, crushed
½ cup tomato paste
3 cups beef broth
1 cup Cynthiana or Norton
Salt and pepper to taste
1 tablespoon butter

In a saucepan, heat the olive oil and then sauté the onions and mushrooms over medium heat until caramelized. Add garlic and tomato paste and cook 15 minutes more. Add broth and simmer for one hour. Add wine and simmer until alcohol evaporates, about 20 minutes. Strain out the solids. Salt and pepper to taste, and add the butter to the sauce.

Jerry and Joannie serve this sauce with meatballs that have a whole clove of garlic hidden inside or with any beef dish like Beef Wellington. Joannie says you can puree the solids into the sauce if you want a more rustic sauce.

WINDRUSH FARM
FARMINGTON

Find vegetables, herbs, and flowers at Windrush Farm.

A big gust of wind literally blew Linda Williams off her feet when she was gardening one day, and the name of her farm was born. At Windrush Farm, you can find heirloom varieties of vegetables, some hybrid varieties picked for flavor, flowers, dried herbs for teas or cooking, spice mixes, natural soil enhancers, and a breeze almost daily. Linda is a Master Gardener and teaches sustainable and organic gardening methods at Mineral Area College. Her organic market garden and stand are a passion.

Each spring, Linda sells vegetable plants grown from seeds in her house at markets. Her plants are healthy and strong, thanks to her special potting soil, which contains minerals and locally made compost. "I've always been into soil," she says. "It's where it all starts."

The plants grown in Linda's system are so popular that she has a reservation program and sells out quickly. During the summer months, she dehydrates herbs. An assortment of small containers hold a rainbow of flavor: apple mint, garlic powder, holy basil, basil, lemon balm, bay leaves, chocolate cherry tomatoes, mixed cherry tomatoes, sweet peppers, and heirloom tomato powder, among other treasures. "It's important to me to help people understand the seasonality of food and to eat seasonally," Linda says.

Preserving the flavors of spring and summer by drying herbs and vegetables is a way to do that and still get variety year-round. Heirloom Tomato Powder from Windrush is made from full-flavored tomatoes dried for use in sauces, soups, stews, breads, cheese dips, eggs, and salad dressings. She recommends rehydrating sweet peppers with boiling water before draining and adding them to a sauté of a few onions, scrambled eggs, and dried basil. "It'll look like a party," she says.

Linda put in raised beds for her plants and, with the help of her brother, Leonard Williams, a sun porch, farm stand, and greenhouse for propagating and selling her products. She has around 1,400 tomato plant starts each spring. Some get planted at Windrush, but most are sold at the Farmington Farmers' Market or on her reservation program. She grows unusual varieties and old ones. "I want the older ladies that have been dreaming about that good, big old tomato taste to be able to get it."

She dries all kinds of vegetables: carrots, green beans, beets that never make it to the market because she likes them in summer soups, and more. She dehydrates herbs such as lemon balm, holy basil, sage, lime mint, apple mint, lemon verbena, chocolate mint, peppermint, and orange mint for tea. She dries culinary herbs such as bay. Linda makes her own recipe for "Soil Food," and instead of chemical fertilizers, she feeds the ground around her plants with what the life in the soil will eat—alfalfa, kelp meal, greensand (glauconite-bearing sandstones), and gypsum. The worms, microorganisms, and little bugs love it and so will your tomato plants, Linda says. "I found my purpose." And you can tell.

Windrush Farm
Linda Williams
3503 Sand Creek Road
Farmington, MO 63640

lwilliam@mineralarea.edu
573-760-1731

Farm Stand
Sundays - Thursdays:
8 a.m. - 6 p.m.

Farmington Farmers' Market
Saturdays:
7 a.m. - 11 a.m.

Polenta with Cherry Tomatoes and Basil
Serves 6

1 quart cold water
1 teaspoon salt
½ cup dehydrated cherry tomatoes
1 cup white or yellow corn meal
1 heaping teaspoon dried basil

2 tablespoons unsalted butter
1 cup grated Italian cheese
   blend or Parmesan cheese
Butter
Olive oil

Pour water into a large (2-quart or larger) saucepan. Add salt and dehydrated cherry tomatoes. Bring to a boil over medium heat. Slowly add corn meal, stirring constantly. When mixture returns to a boil, cover pan and reduce heat to medium low. Cook, stirring occasionally, until mixture is very thick and cherry tomatoes are soft. Stir in the basil and turn the heat off. Then, add the butter and cheese, mixing well.

Pour the mixture into a well-buttered 6x9-inch pan. Hold until the next day for the best flavor, or when cooled, cut into squares and fry the squares in a small amount of butter or olive oil until brown on both sides. Serve topped with pasta sauce, or a sprinkle of grated Parmesan cheese, or right out of the pot as a side dish.

JONES HERITAGE FARMS AND MARKET
JACKSON

Visit the red barn with old-style food at Jones Heritage Farms and Market.

If you're reading *Savor Missouri*, you have a weakness for tasty foods. If you also have a weakness for red barns on country roads, you'll love Jones Heritage Farms and Market. The Market in Cape Girardeau County has country appeal, fresh hormone-free and antibiotic-free pork, beef, chicken, eggs, and produce, and its own restaurant—all housed in a red barn. The tables have red-checked cloths, and the windows look out over a deck and pond complete with gliding swans. In the summers, there is often music. The menu changes depending on what the farm has on offer and the chef's personal selections, but if you get a chance, try the honey-glazed Berkshire pork chops with lavender, green beans with bacon, polenta made with fresh milk, Parmesan, and chipotle.

Jones Heritage Farms has a preference for old-style foods—those raised naturally with sustainability in mind and using environmentally friendly methods to control pests.

Gerry Jones, his family, and his staff like and raise heritage breed animals for the flavor intensity. The reason these breeds have fallen out of favor, Gerry says, is because they don't stand up well in mass production facilities, but are worth the effort to raise for taste. Gerry also chooses vegetables from heirloom seed varieties, those seeds with ancestors dating 100-plus years, for his potatoes, tomatoes, asparagus, lettuce, carrots, and corn.

Produce not used in the Market or restaurant is sold wholesale to restaurants in St. Louis. The flavors of heritage-breed animals, heirloom-variety produce, hormone-free eggs, and other staples from nearby farmers are sold in the on-site market. Come taste for yourself in Cape Girardeau County.

Jones Heritage Farms
5739 State Highway W
Jackson, MO 63755

www.jonesheritagefarms.com
573-332-7447

Mondays - Fridays:
10 a.m. - 6 p.m.
Saturdays:
8 a.m. - 4 p.m.

Hours may vary seasonally; call ahead to check.

MEIER HORSE SHOE PINES
JACKSON

Find lamb, a Christmas shop, plus your Christmas tree at Meier Horse Shoe Pines.

It's a family affair at Meier Horse Shoe Pines near Jackson. It's hard to know where to begin: horses, trees, lamb, a Christmas shop. It's all here, and all the Meiers take part.

In 1983, Teresa and Steve Meier planted their first Scotch, white, and Virginia pines, as well as spruce and fir trees. Then, they added a twist: Belgian draft horses and a wagon to take customers out to the field to pick their trees. Steve's father farmed with horses and mules, and that memory, along with the old harnesses Steve kept oiled each year, came together in Meier Horse Shoe Pines. The horses, beautifully golden and very, very large, toss their heads, eat corn right off the cob, and generally charm anyone nearby. Most of the Meier tree sales for the year happen in six days: Thanksgiving weekend and the weekend just after. The wagon rides are a big hit with visitors.

Son Ben helps with the farm, growing corn, beans, barley, and producing hay for the horses. In his seventh-grade year, Ben's 4-H project gave him another passion: sheep. After one season watching Ben, Teresa knew the sheep were on the farm to stay. Ben now raises lamb for sale to individuals by arrangement in mid- to late summer.

The animals on Meier Horse Shoe Pines are raised on the farm's own feed, and Ben's ear corn replaces soybean hulls used in commercial feeds for fillers.

The farm also has one other unusual feature: the Christmas Shop at Horse Shoe Pines. Thousands of decorations for the holidays are on hand and glittering, drawing happy repeat customers each year. Teresa has fresh wreaths, too.

From left: Teresa, Steve, Ben, Shelby, and Charlie Meier.

Meier Horse Shoe Pines
2146 County Road 330
Jackson, MO 63755

www.meierhorseshoepines.com
573-243-5501

Christmas Shop
November weekends
Fridays - Sundays:
1 p.m. - 5 p.m.

Thanksgiving - Christmas
Tuesdays - Fridays:
1 p.m. - 5 p.m.
Saturdays:
10 a.m. - 5 p.m.
Sundays:
11 a.m. - 5 p.m.

Tree Farm
Thanksgiving weekend and
the following weekend
or call before driving

Pastured lamb
by arrangement

Lamb Marinade
Makes about 1⅓ cups

⅔ cup lemon juice
½ cup brown sugar
¼ cup prepared mustard
¼ cup soy sauce
¼ cup olive oil
2 teaspoons garlic, minced
1 teaspoon ground ginger
1 teaspoon salt
½ teaspoon black pepper, freshly cracked
Lamb chops or cubed lamb for kabobs
Green pepper and pineapple chunks for kabobs

In a bowl, mix the lemon juice, brown sugar, mustard, soy sauce, olive oil, garlic, ginger, salt, and pepper. Place the lamb in a shallow container. Pour the lemon juice mixture over the lamb. Cover and marinate in the refrigerator 8 hours or overnight.

Preheat an outdoor grill to medium heat. Drain marinade into a saucepan and bring it to a boil. Reduce heat to low and simmer, whisking constantly, until slightly thickened.

For kabobs: Cut lamb into 1-inch chunks and thread onto skewers with green pepper and pineapple chunks (if desired).

Lightly oil the grill grate. Over indirect heat, grill the lamb chops or kabobs, brushing with the marinade, turning to cook all sides, to a minimum internal temperature of 145°F.

BEGGS' PIONEER MARKET AND ORCHARD
JACKSON

Pick your own peaches and apples at Pioneer Market.

The sense of family story is strong at Begg's Pioneer Market and Orchard near Jackson. The family first planted apple trees here in 1948, and there's been pick-your-own apples, and later peaches, ever since. "There are still a few of the original trees we planted in the front yard," LaDonia Beggs says. Though the orchard, managed by son Stanley, has had years in the 1970s and 80s when 15 to 20 semi-trucks would load up with fruit during the season, apples and peaches are now mostly sold off the tree or in Pioneer Market nearby.

There is a straw maze throughout October, too. You can choose your pumpkin out of a 10-acre patch and drift through a tall grass maze or even an apple bin maze. At nearby Pioneer Market, run by LaDonia's brother-in-law, Sam, you can choose your apples out of a bin, purchase apple butter made in kettles, and pick out apple pies that many folks order in advance. LaDonia makes about 35 apple, peach, and pumpkin pies per week to keep up with demand. The Market began in 1952 as a roadside stand. Today, it's filled with melons, sweet corn, tomatoes, apples, and peaches sourced locally when possible. When you visit, you might find one or another of LaDonia's family, daughter-in-law Heather or niece Sarah, perhaps, helping.

Beginning around July 1, one variety of peaches or another is ripe and ready for customers. Bright Star peaches ripen first, and every week to week-and-a-half another variety comes on until mid-September when Autumn Prince finishes the season. Then, it's apple time. Next, after pick-your-own winds down, the family begins putting together gift baskets. The gift basket tradition began for the Beggs in 1968 and has grown to a significant portion of their business in late fall through Christmas.

Heather Beggs (left) and Sarah Beggs Cook

Sam Beggs

Beggs' Pioneer Market and Orchard
2008 W. Jackson Boulevard
Jackson, MO 63755

pioneerorchard@aol.com
573-243-8476

Farm and Store
Mondays - Saturdays:
8 a.m. - 6 p.m.
Sundays:
11 a.m. - 5 p.m.

LaDonia and Stanley Beggs

Danish Pastry Apple Bars
LaDonia Beggs, Pioneer Apple Orchard; makes 3 dozen bars

2-½ cups and 3 tablespoons sifted flour, divided
1 teaspoon salt
1 cup shortening
1 egg yoke
Milk
½ cup sliced almonds, with extra optional for topping
8-10 tart apples, peeled and sliced
¾ to 1 cup sugar
1 teaspoon cinnamon
1 egg white
Powdered sugar glaze or frosting

Preheat oven to 350°F. Combine flour and salt. Cut in the shortening. Set aside. Beat the egg yolk in a cup and add enough milk to make ⅔ cup of liquid. Stir egg mixture into the flour mixture. Roll half of the dough on a floured board into a 17x12-inch rectangle. Put rolled-out dough on a large cookie sheet and then sprinkle with the almonds. Next, in a large bowl, toss sliced apples with flour. Spread over the almond layer. In a bowl, combine sugar and cinnamon and sprinkle over the apples. Roll out the remaining dough and cover the apples. Beat the egg white until frothy, brush on the top crust. Bake for 50 minutes. Remove from oven and while warm, drizzle with powdered sugar glaze, or when cool use powdered sugar icing. Add almonds on top, if desired.

BREEZY RIDGE ALPACA FARM
PERRYVILLE

Please don't eat the alpaca. Or the wool.

Breezy Ridge is not about food or wine, but I couldn't resist a stop at Connie Blechle's alpaca farm shop. Connie felt like a jack-of-all-trades and master of none until she came across alpacas. Now, her days are filled with fiber. Connie cares for a herd of 20 Suri alpacas and harvests the wool each May. She cleans, cards, spins the wool, and sells the yarn, specialty scarves, hats, and sweaters from her farm shop near Perryville, at craft fairs, or more recently, online.

When you drive into the Blechle farm, you notice the gate system Connie uses to keep the males and females separated until breeding time. The farmland slips away from the house, and trees line the horizon. It's a beautiful, peaceful, and curious place to find the long-lashed, inquisitive alpacas. Wait just a moment and Connie will call out nearly all their names and explain their personalities. She only parts with stock if it is to people she can maintain contact with to check on her animals after the sale. Mostly, she is happiest harvesting the wool to make textiles or to sell outright.

Connie's farm shop is a tactile experience. The wool is glossy and soft. Her creations—lacy shawls, scarves, mittens, hats, and tiny alpaca dolls—are neatly arranged and displayed. She tends to like the natural wool colors that already have a surprising range from black and silver-gray, to white, brown, and maroon, over the dyed wools, but offers both. Trace your fingers through a skein, or ask to feel a bat of carded wool and feel the wonder of alpaca.

Connie checks on Trixie, Cover Girl (CG), Max Factor, Fiona, Pearl, Flame, Thunder, Sonic, Magic, Silver, Bourbon, Arctic Blast (Artie), Eira, Gucci, Miranda, and the rest every morning. She cleans the barn and waters her animals, all while speaking to them gently. Each one has a distinct personality that Connie knows, and each one has large eyes peering out from under flossy bangs. Fiona is so friendly she likes her stomach rubbed. Connie feeds them orchard grass hay or brome at the rate of about two pounds per day per animal. They get alpaca grain with extra vitamins each evening and love carrots as a treat. Six to eight animals can live on an acre comfortably. The farm is open for visitors by appointment.

Breezy Ridge Alpaca
908 PCR 810
Perryville, MO 63775

www.breezyridgealpacas.com
info@breezyridgealpacas.com
573-547-2217

Hours by appointment

STONIE'S SAUSAGE SHOP
PERRYVILLE

Stonie's Sausage Shop still uses unique early recipes.

Stanislaus (Stonie) Wibbenmeyer started it. He worked with a Perryville butcher in the early 1900s as a boy. Then, in 1930, he began working for Duerr Meat Market and eventually managed the business until it closed in 1959. That same year, he built his own building in Perryville. Since then, it's been a progression of Wibbenmeyers at the helm of Stonies Sausage Shop.

First, it was Stonie's son, Don Wibbenmeyer, in 1962, then his grandson, Roger, by 1975, and now, Roger's son, Tyson, is part of the business. The facility has grown to 15,000 square feet, and the family handles retail as well as wholesale sales and a host of private label business across the country.

The shop is filled with tasty meats: sausages, specialty burgers, wild rice and mushroom-stuffed pork chops, snack sticks, hams, ribs, and hamburger—more than 200 products and 30-plus bratwurst in all. To create the flavors in the bratwurst and other products, there is an entire wall of shelves devoted to spices: dried onion, pepper, dill, chorizo, chili, maple, apple, coriander, fennel, whole mustard, paprika, special blends, and marinades such as lemon garlic and sun-dried tomato basil.

The family has developed so many recipes over the years Roger doesn't attempt to count them, but some of the early flavors still work well. "There was something unique about those first recipes," Roger says. "We are still running recipes for bacon, bologna, summer sausage, and pork loin we had in the beginning. The machinery is different, but we work the same as my grandfather did back then. He gave us a really good base."

The retail store offers gift boxes in the late fall. Grandson Dane put together 4,000 to 5,000 last season and is ready to help again. Dane's younger sister, Zoey, is showing interest. It's the fifth generation rising for Stonie's.

Stonie's Sausage Shop
1507 Edgemont Boulevard
Perryville, MO 63775

www.shopstonies.com
contact@shopstonies.com
888-546-2540

Retail and Lunch Counter
Mondays - Friday:
7:30 a.m. - 6:30 p.m.
Saturdays:
7:30 a.m. - 4:30 p.m.
Sundays:
10:30 a.m. - 2:30 p.m.

Tyson, Barb, and Roger Wibbenmeyer

Bacon Wrapped Chicken Roll
Serves 4

4 boneless skinless chicken breasts
Stonie's Rosemary Basil Thyme Seasoning, enough to sprinkle
1 cup chive and onion cream cheese
4 pieces Stonie's Hickory Smoked Bacon

Flatten chicken breast to about ¼-inch thickness with meat tenderizer. Sprinkle Stonie's Rosemary Basil Thyme Seasoning on both sides of chicken breast. Spread cream cheese on one side of chicken breast. Roll chicken breast so the cream cheese is on the inside of roll. Wrap rolled chicken breast with Stonie's Hickory Smoked Bacon.

Place chicken breast in covered baking dish. Bake at 375°F degrees for 35 minutes then uncover and bake an additional 5 minutes to allow the bacon to brown. The internal temperature should be 160°F degrees.

CAVE VINEYARD
STE. GENEVIEVE

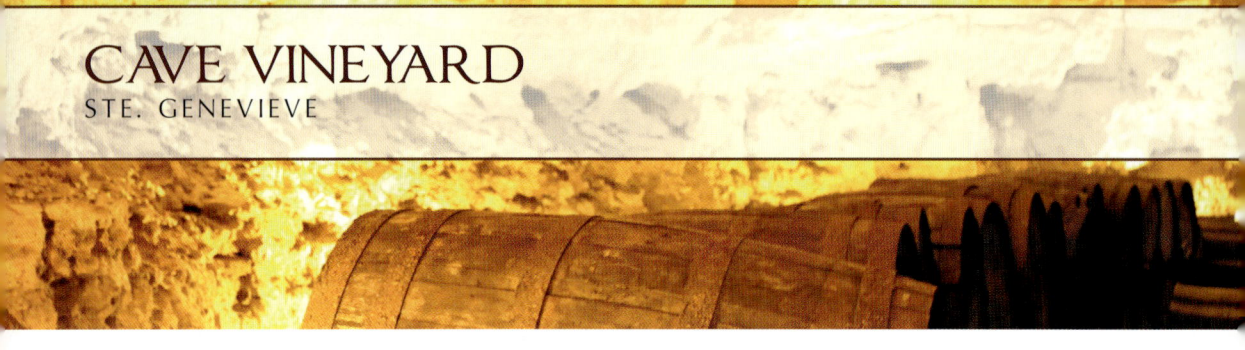

Cave Vineyard has its own natural limestone cavern.

To Marty and Mary Jo Strussion, wine is a family affair. The couple decided to retire in the rolling hills outside of Ste. Genevieve, found the perfect property in 1995 and the perfect recipe for keeping their family involved in each other and close: wine. The couple planted their first grapes in 2001 and now, with 15 acres in vines and a yearly production of about 6,000 gallons per year the Strussions are happy to say that their four daughters, three sons-in-law, and nine grandchildren help at the vineyard. The Cave Vineyard grapes, Chardonel, Traminette, Chambourcin, and Cynthiana/Norton, were first harvested in 2003. The winery now grows Vignoles, too.

The Strussions' vineyard has its own natural limestone cave that is available for picnics. At the entrance, the cave is 100 feet across and 35 feet high, and it stretches back into the earth about 900 feet. It has a natural temperature of 58 degrees Fahrenheit—something Marty hopes to put to use by storing wine barrels in partitioned space. Events can also be scheduled there. Visitors walk the 200 yards on a paved path to view the cave or take a shuttle on weekends. A Frenchman following Native American trails in the mid-1700s found the cave, which was later a source for the bat guano (nitrates) needed for making black gunpowder. It is so much a part of the hills that even the massive New Madrid earthquakes of 1811 and 1812 did nothing to its structure. Now, the expansive space, with its seawater markings from 30,000 years ago, is a cool oasis for sipping.

Up the hill, the Cave Vineyard tasting room is filled with light, and the view from the porch offers peacefully swaying trees and gentle hills. There's an outdoor pavilion, a lake, and Mary Jo's freshly baked bread on Saturday mornings in the summer season. A biscotti bar has recently been added so visitors can try different wines with biscotti selections such as almond, chocolate cayenne, anise, and mascarpone and dark cherry.

Marty enjoys learning the chemistry behind different wines and likes talking about wine-making with visitors. "You're taking something mother nature basically gives you and creating a unique product." Downstairs, you can see his process: his office has wine-making supplies, beakers, and charts, the crowded desk the result of his analysis of a recent harvest.

Mary Jo tackles the winery's beautiful floral gardens outside the tasting room and patio. Hummingbirds and visitors alike love the colors surrounding the porch. In the vineyard, she enjoys the tactile work of training and tying up the vines, as well as pruning, "Each vine is different so it's not monotonous," she says, smiling.

It's family, however, that they both mention as their favorite part of the vineyard. As we walk through the seating area inside, Mary Jo pulls me over to see the family photos: "This is what it's all about, right here."

Cave Vineyard
21124 Cave Road
Ste. Genevieve, MO 63670

www.cavevineyard.com
jostrussion@cavevineyard.com
573-543-5284

Summer, April - October
Daily:
10 a.m. - 6 p.m.

Winter, November - March
Daily:
10 a.m. - 5 p.m.

Marty and Mary Jo Strussion

Norton Brownies
Makes 36 brownies

1-½ cups flour
2 teaspoons baking powder
½ teaspoon salt
½ cup butter, softened
1-¼ cups sugar
2 eggs

3 squares (3 ounces) unsweetened chocolate, melted and cooled
1 teaspoon vanilla
1 cup Norton wine
1 cup chopped walnuts (optional)

For frosting:
3 tablespoons butter
2 squares (2 ounces) unsweetened chocolate
¼ cup milk and extra as needed to thin
3 cups powdered sugar

Preheat oven to 350°F. Grease a 15x10x1-inch baking pan. Combine flour, baking powder and salt, set aside. In another bowl, beat butter for 30 seconds; add sugar and beat until fluffy. Add eggs, chocolate, and vanilla; beat well. Add dry ingredients and Norton wine alternately to the chocolate mixture. Stir in walnuts. Turn batter into the pan and bake for 18 to 20 minutes. Cool on a wire rack. Frost if desired.

Chocolate Frosting
Over medium heat on the stovetop, heat butter, chocolate, and milk until chocolate melts. Stir in powdered sugar. Thin with milk if needed to spreading consistency.

CHARLEVILLE VINEYARD
STE. GENEVIEVE

Rustic 1860s log cabin adds to welcome at Charleville Vineyard, Winery & Microbrewery.

Above Saline Creek Valley in western Ste. Genevieve County is a rustic winery that could be easy to miss. But don't let yourself. As you drive through thick Missouri woods to arrive, you feel as if you might be a *bit* off the beaten track. The land opens up then, and you get your first glimpse of why this spot is popular with visitors. Joal and Jack Russell opened Charleville Winery tasting room in June 2003, but they had already been growing grapes for several years for bulk sale. The Russells wanted to have a retirement project and fell in love with the land. What they created is a lovely spot with a relaxed atmosphere. You can stay awhile here.

After their first season of selling their own wines, the Russells were pleasantly surprised with customer reaction: "We needed to buy some tables and chairs," Joal says. They did more than that, creating a tasting room with cedar plank logs and bringing in an 1860s log cabin, moved from St. Mary, Missouri, to be a bed and breakfast Joal manages on weekends. The cabin's exterior is original and though floors inside were replaced, the building maintains its original charm.

They also opened Charleville Brewing Co. in 2004 and now have a full time brewmaster and winemaker, Tony Saballa. The small-batch brewing totals around 600 barrels a year of ales, lagers, and seasonal beers, and they find it hard sometimes not to run out due to demand. The winery now produces about 1,000 cases of wine each year.

Charleville is host to fireflies and Missouri views each season. Make your way through the woods to visit.

Joal Russell

**Charleville Vineyard
Winery and Microbrewery**
16937 Boyd Road
Ste. Genevieve, MO 63670

www.charlevillevineyard.com
573-756-4537

Tasting Room
Wednesdays - Thursdays:
Noon - 6 p.m.
Fridays - Sundays:
11 a.m. - 6 p.m.

Roasted Chicken Basted with Chardonel
Serves 4

Whole chicken, rinsed and patted dry
4 cloves garlic, minced or mashed, divided
1 teaspoon salt
½ teaspoon black pepper
1 teaspoon tarragon, crushed
½-1 cup Charleville Barrel Fermented Chardonel
Rice or risotto

Preheat oven to 375°F. Rub cavity of the chicken with 2 cloves crushed garlic and salt. Next mix the remaining garlic, black pepper, and tarragon in a small cup or bowl and rub the outer skin of the chicken with this mixture. Roast chicken in a cast-iron Dutch oven for about 1 hour and 15 minutes or until golden brown. While chicken is roasting, pour ½ to 1 cup of Charleville Chardonel over chicken. Baste frequently using a large spoon or baster. Serve with rice or risotto using the chicken juice as a sauce for the rice.

Chardonel is also a great baster for turkey.

Tony Saballa

87

CHAUMETTE WINERY
STE. GENEVIEVE

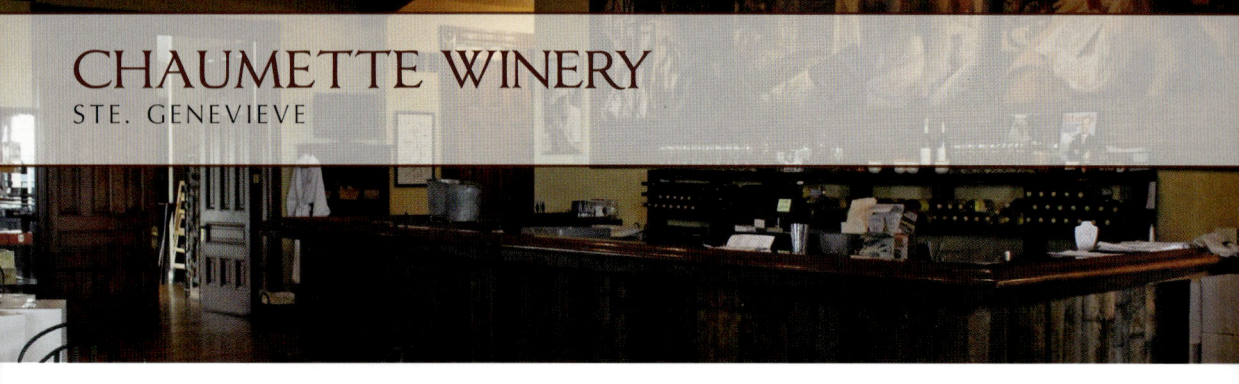

Chaumette Winery is an oasis in French Colonial style.

It's a scenic drive out through gently sloping hills and rustling trees to the Chaumette Winery and Grapevine Grill outside of Ste. Genevieve.

The winery's graceful entry carries the mark of people who care about what they do. Hank and Jackie Johnson, owners of Chaumette Winery, created an oasis here. The vista is lovely, abutting 10,000 acres of Mark Twain National Forrest. The buildings are vertical log replications of 1780s colonial French buildings like those in Ste. Genevieve, and the wines are a delight.

None of this comes by chance, though getting into the wine business itself was a slow roll of the dice for Hank. Prior to 1990, Hank and Jackie came out to the area for weekends to get away from their work in St. Louis: Jackie as an attorney and Hank as a helicopter insurance broker. Then, a farm came up for sale. By 1992, Hank was getting tired of mowing those farm fields and planted grapes, which he sold to other wineries for two years. He had the itch by then, and Chaumette Winery was born.

Wines here run a scale of taste that enthusiasts will appreciate. Hank's passion for viticulture engages his days, and it is this focus that produces several strong selections from his list. Unlike many Missouri wineries, Chaumette does 65 percent of its wine sales in dry wines such as Chambourcin, Assemblage, an unoaked Chardonel, and a Reserve Chardonel. Another 15 percent of their sales are in semi-dry varieties. "We're in the business of education," Hank says. It's important, he says, that the same grape, grown in the same place, can have completely different outcomes. "Seventy-five percent of what ends up in your glass happens in the vineyard, both in style and quality."

As Hank drives to his wine cellar, he stops to talk with an employee in a pickup truck alongside the road. In his fleece vest and long-sleeved button-up shirt, Hank talks about daily operations and seems relaxed yet exacting. Through the course of an afternoon, he gets phone calls about water tanks and ice machine deliveries. As he walks through the facilities, he explains why he believes in Missouri regional grapes: California varietals emerge too early here. "Last year in January we had five days of 60°F weather, then it was cold again, then warm." He talks about the experimental wine he hopes to develop: a white wine with the healthy properties of a red. "Forty to forty-five percent of people like white wine. What if you could do that?"

A similar sense of exploring for the best results comes from Chaumette's restaurant, the Grapevine Grill, led by Chef Adam Lambay and Sous Chef Dan Linza. The interior of the building has high-beamed ceilings and wide plank wood floors. A comfortable dining room joins the tasting area, and menu items vary by season, though Chef Adam is likely to create dishes with Asian as well as American influences.

Dan's experience in the West Indies taught him how to creatively use sugar cane, coconut milk, and mango to create subtle and flavorful dishes. His jerk chicken includes an onion base with brown sugar, cinnamon, thyme, nutmeg, allspice, ginger, garlic, habanero pepper, cilantro, and ghost chilis. Though ghost chilis are the hottest chilis in the world, the taste range of Dan's chicken perks up the tongue with cilantro first, then opens to the nutmeg before the heat comes onto your tongue. It is surprisingly easy to eat, even for those who prefer medium-heat chilis, and definitely tasty.

Another draw to Chaumette is its chapel, St. Vincent's In-the-Vineyard, a Mission Church of the Episcopal Diocese of Missouri, transported in pieces here and carefully reconstructed when its original site near St. Louis was marked for housing development.

Hank was pleased to save St. Vincent's In-the-Vineyard. Its sturdy frame exterior is charming nestled in the trees, and there is a welcoming feel to the plain space inside. Hank ensured that every door, window, light fixture, and communion rail was put back together as it was originally. The chapel was completed at Chaumette in October 2003. In 2007, an all-faith service in the Episcopal tradition was begun.

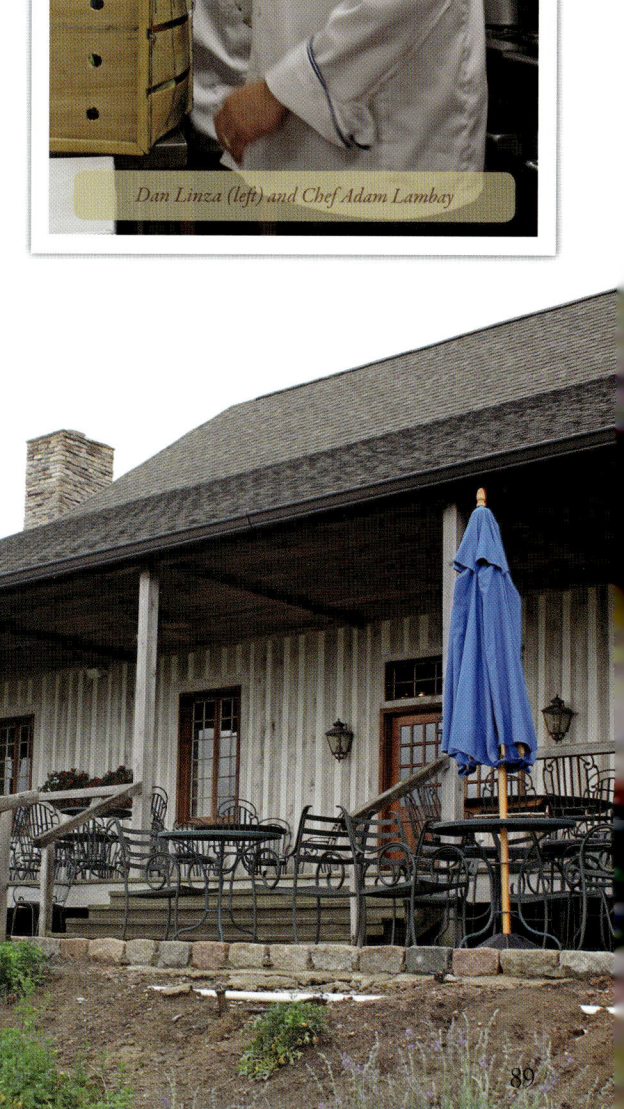

Dan Linza (left) and Chef Adam Lambay

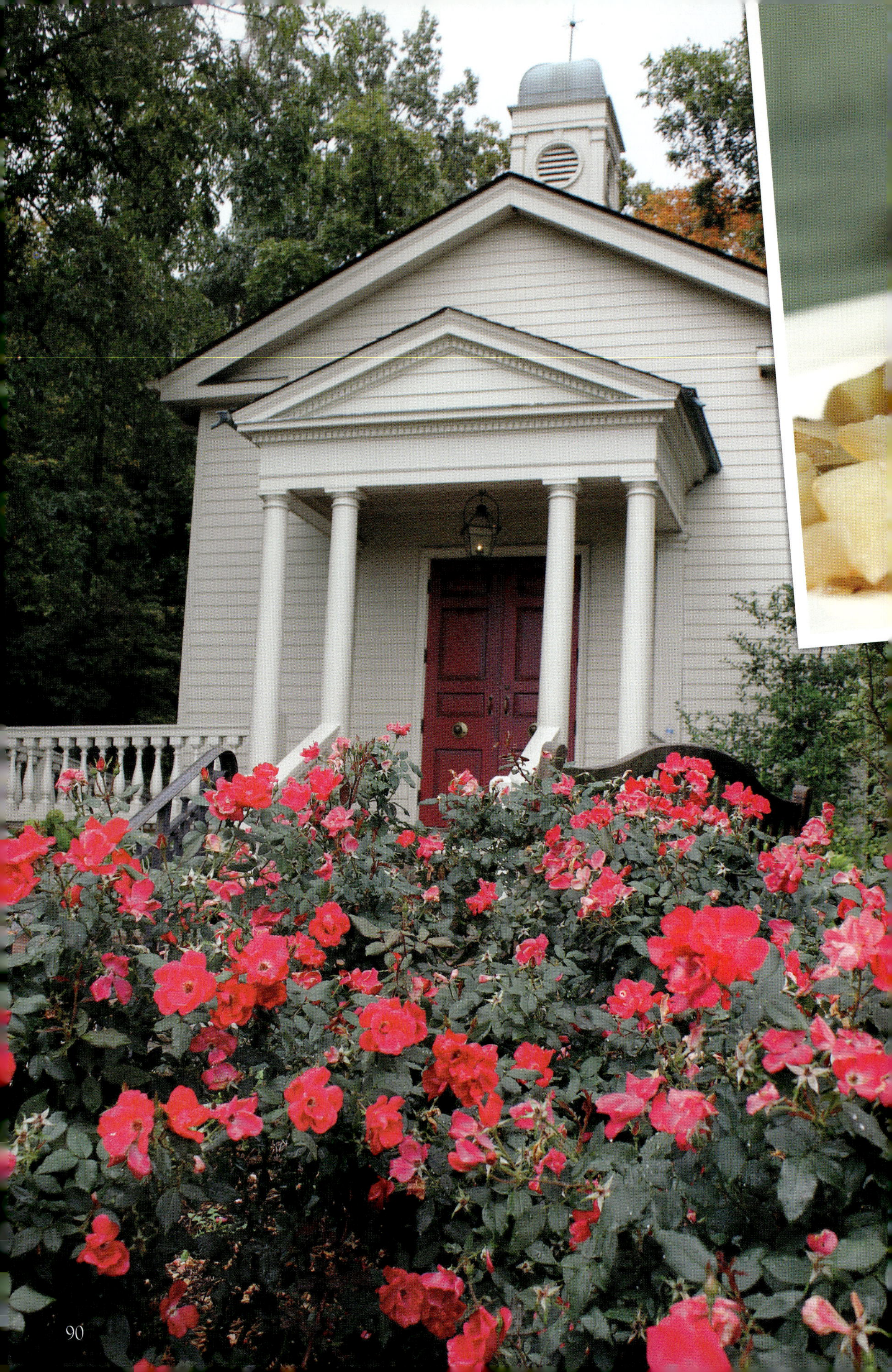

Chaumette Vineyards & Winery and Grapevine Grill
24345 State Route WW
Ste. Genevieve, MO 63670

www.chaumette.com
573-747-1000

April through August
Tasting room
Sundays and Wednesdays:
Noon - 5 p.m.
Thursdays - Saturdays:
Noon - 6 p.m.

September through October
Tasting room
Wednesdays:
11 a.m. - 5 p.m.
Thursdays - Sundays:
11 a.m. - 7 p.m.

Grapevine Grill
Wednesdays - Sundays:
Noon - 3 p.m.
Sunday harvest dinner:
5 p.m. - 8:30 p.m. last order
Thursdays - Saturdays:
5 p.m. - 8:30 p.m. last order

Winter hours vary, call or check website for more information.

Chaumette Chicken
Chef Adam Lambay

For the chicken
- 1 tablespoon fresh thyme, chopped
- 1 teaspoon fresh rosemary, chopped
- 3 tablespoons fresh parsley, Italian or curly leaf, chopped
- 5 pounds chicken, split and quartered
- ¼ cup olive oil
- 4 cloves garlic, minced
- 1 tablespoon kosher or sea salt
- ½ teaspoon ground black pepper

For the braise
- 4 tablespoons butter
- ½ pound bacon, thick cut, diced
- 1 large yellow or white onion, julienned
- ½ cup garlic, fresh chopped
- 2 cups mushrooms, quartered (crimini or your personal favorite)
- ½ bottle Chaumette Chambourcin Wine
- 1 bay leaf
- ½ teaspoon fresh rosemary, stemmed and chopped
- 2 tablespoons fresh Italian parsley, chopped
- 1 quart chicken stock
- 1 pound new red potatoes, sliced
- 1 turnip, peeled and sliced
- 1 teaspoon fresh thyme, stemmed and chopped

Heat a large roasting pan on medium heat. Meanwhile, for the chicken, blend or puree the olive oil, garlic, salt, and pepper together and then stir in the herbs. Coat the chicken with the oil mixture. Place the chicken immediately in the hot roasting pan. Generously brown both sides of the meat and remove from the pan.

Then for the braise, add the butter and allow to melt. Add the bacon. Brown the bacon and render out almost all of its fat. With a wooden spoon or similar utensil, scrape the bottom of the pan to remove or loosen the brown bits. Add the onion and sauté until translucent but not brown. Add the garlic. When the edges of the onions start to brown, add the mushrooms. The mushrooms will sweat out a lot of moisture—allow all of that to cook off. When the pan is dry, deglaze with the Chaumette Chambourcin. Bring the wine to a boil and let it reduce by at least half.

Now return the chicken to the pan skin side up. Add the bay leaf, other herbs, and the stock. Bring to boil and then drop in the potatoes and turnip. Place in an oven at 350°F. Roast uncovered for about one hour or until the legs are fork tender. Remove the roasting pan from the oven. Remove the chicken from the pan. Bring the sauce back to boil. Reduce to the desired consistency. Check the salt and pepper.

CROWN VALLEY WINERY AND BREWERY
STE. GENEVIEVE

Crown Valley hosts a winery, brewery, distillery, and a herd of 400 bison.

They call it Crown Country, and once you visit you can see why. a farm that raises 400 head of bison as well as 2,000 Black Angus beef cattle. The winery, which produces 30,000 cases of wine per year, was established in 2002.

Visitors to the winery can browse the wine shop, walk through the stainless steel tanks of the fermentation room, and visit the tasting area. Views from the tasting area and decks encompass Crown Valley land.

Alwyn J. Dippenaar, a native of Cape Town, South Africa, is the winery's master winemaker. After training in South Africa, Oregon, New Zealand, and Western Australia, he decided he wanted to learn more about how American wines were developed and chose Missouri. "You learn more about wine making here because you work with many more (weather) situations than California."

That challenge and the process from field to glass is what keeps him interested. "I express the vineyard. It's a transformation." His goal at Crown Valley? To take on the Missouri Norton grape.

"I can stay here all day and just work. I enjoy going through the whole process. Every day I make split-second decisions (about the wines). Sometimes they're right, sometimes they're wrong. You go with your feelings." That creativity is what draws Alwyn to winemaking. "I wouldn't want to do anything else. I like to say the wine makes itself, you just control the environment." In summer 2013, Alwyn will release a new velvet Muscat.

Crown Valley is also a distiller as well as a craft beer producer, making ales, lagers, and a porter. Tours and tastings are available.

Sparkling Peaches & Cream
Serves 4

1 can (16 ounces) peach slices, chilled
½ cup unsweetened pineapple juice, chilled
1 egg
1 tablespoon sugar
1 tablespoon lemon juice
1 teaspoon vanilla
4 ice cubes
1 cup light cream
½ cup sparkling mineral water or carbonated water, chilled
1 cup Crown Valley Chardonel Wine, chilled
Sliced almonds (optional)

In a blender, combine the undrained peach slices, pineapple juice, egg, sugar, lemon juice, vanilla, and ice cubes. Cover and blend until smooth. Stir in cream; slowly pour sparkling water and Chardonel wine down the side of the container. Stir gently with an up-and-down motion to mix. Pour into 4 chilled glasses. If desired, garnish each serving with sliced almonds.

Berry Frappe
Serves 4

3 cups frozen loose-pack raspberries or strawberries, divided
1 (12-ounce) can carbonated crème soda
1 (8-ounce) carton plain yogurt
½ of a 6-ounce can (⅓ cup) frozen lemonade concentrate, thawed
¼ cup sugar
2 cups carbonated water, chilled
1 cup Crown Valley Riesling Wine, chilled

In a blender, place half of the berries, soda, yogurt, frozen concentrate, and sugar. Cover; blend until berries are pureed and sugar is dissolved. Pour into a 13x9x2-inch pan. Repeat blending the remaining ingredients except carbonated water and Riesling; pour into pan. Cover; freeze 3 hours or until firm. Use a fork to break up the frozen mixture. Put half of the frozen mixture in a blender. Add 1 cup of the carbonated water and ½ cup of the Riesling. Cover and blend until frothy. Repeat. Pour into chilled glasses.

BREWING A MISSOURI LEGEND

Brewer Jim Kron

German Beer Spread
Serves 12

- 2 cups (8 ounces) sharp cheddar cheese, shredded
- 2 cups (8 ounces) Swiss cheese, shredded
- 1 teaspoon Worcestershire sauce
- ½ teaspoon dry mustard
- 1 clove garlic, minced
- ½ cup Crown Valley Brewery Plowboy Porter Craft Beer
- Assorted rye or pumpernickel crackers, breadsticks, baguettes, Bavarian pretzels, or bread rounds

Bring cheese to room temperature; place in a food processor bowl fitted with metal blade. Add Worcestershire sauce, mustard, and garlic. Pulse until combined. Add Plowboy Porter and process until smooth, 2 to 3 mintues. Pack in jars or containers; refrigerate overnight to blend flavors. Bring to room temperature and serve with crackers, breadsticks, baguettes, pretzels, or bread rounds.

Winemaker Alwyn J. Dippenaar

Crown Valley Winery
23589 State Route WW
Ste. Genevieve, MO 63670

Crown Valley Brewery
13326 State Route F
Ste. Genevieve, MO 63670

www.crownvalleywinery.com
866-207-9463

Winery
April through October
Wednesdays - Fridays:
11 a.m. - 6 p.m.
Saturdays - Sundays:
11 a.m. - 7 p.m.

November through March
Wednesdays - Sundays:
11 a.m. - 5 p.m.

Brewery
April through October
Wednesdays - Thursdays:
11a.m. - 6p.m.
Fridays:
11 a.m. - 7 p.m.
Saturdays - Sundays:
11 a.m. - 8 p.m.

November through January
Wednesdays - Sundays:
11 a.m. - 6 p.m.

January through March
Wednesdays - Sundays:
11 a.m. - 5 p.m.

ECKENFELS FARMS
STE. GENEVIEVE

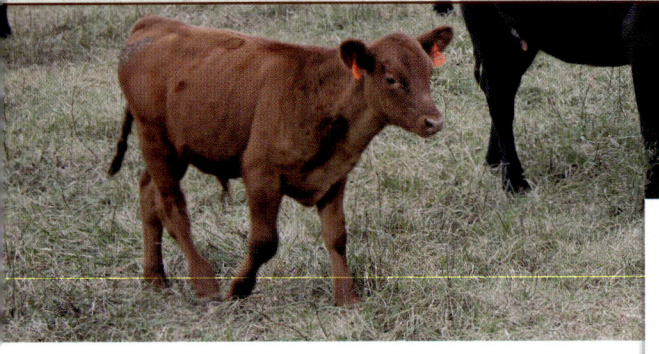

Eckenfels' grass-fed beef thrive in Ste. Genevieve County.

Bob and Sue Eckenfels know beef. And they choose grass-fed with no grain supplements. The couple were both raised on cattle farms near their Ste. Genevieve County home. Their farm, established in 1851 and designated as a century farm, is now in its fifth generation. They were awarded the Environmental Stewardship Award in 2009 by the National Cattlemen's Foundation Association for the way they care for their cattle and land.

What you notice driving along the fences of Eckenfels Farms is grasses shifting in the breeze. Bob uses intensive grazing and rotational pasture techniques to raise grass-fed beef. The pastures are fescue-based with clover. Bob sometimes plants millet, Sudan grass, and rye as supplements. The farm also supports native Little Blue Stem and Big Blue Stem grasses, Indian warm season grasses, and switch grass to allow green pastures during the hottest days of summer when the fescue does not grow. As Bob drives toward his barn, we pass an old granary, chicken house, brooder house, and more.

"Someone once said this is the land of buildings," Bob laughs. "You never actually take one down."

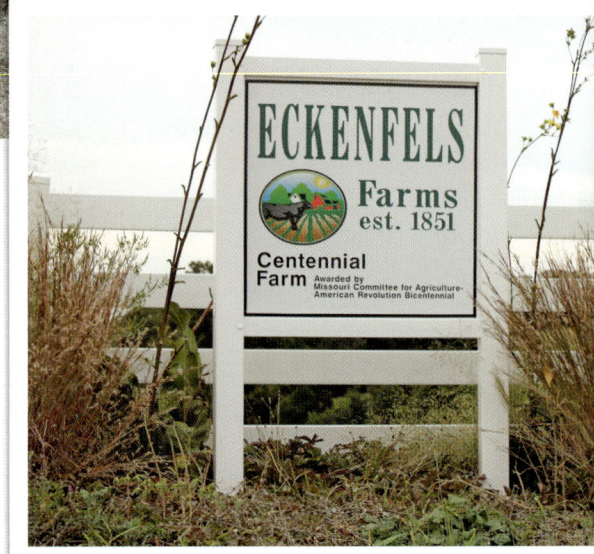

The farm has been in operation since 1851, and a lot has been developed here over the years.

Besides raising quality meat for her family, Sue thinks the best part of farming is raising children that don't sit in front of a television learning to be materialistic. Their youngest, Emily, takes care of the chickens in addition to finding other things to do outside. Their two older girls, Michelle and Kayla, have helped while growing up, and their son, Matthew, now works with Bob. For Bob, the best part of farming is the daily pleasure of farm life: "It's in your blood. That first baby calf in the spring is really something to see."

Front row, from left: Emily, Sue, and Bob Eckenfels; back row: Matthew and Kayla Eckenfels; Michelle, Leah, and David Champion

Eckenfels Farms
19075 Highway 32
St. Genevieve, MO 63670

www.eckenfelsfarms.com
573-883-0337

Call for an appointment or visit these farmers' markets:

Soulard Market, St. Louis
Farmington Farmers' Market
Crystal City Farmers' Market

97

COUNTY LINE FARM
ST. MARY

Try the sweet potatoes, squash, and dozens of other vegetables at County Line Farm.

The vegetable choices get specific at County Line Farm near St. Mary: red-orange Georgia Jet, copper-orange Beauregard, white O'Henry, purple-striped Velvet. And that's just the sweet potatoes. Clyde Bruckerhoff provides fresh vegetables to anyone stopping at his stand at the county line between Perry and Ste. Genevieve counties or at area farmers' markets. His vegetables also appear on restaurant menus in the surrounding area and St. Louis.

The stand has tall dried stalks of corn bundled around two edges to enclose the space. There are tables of fresh vegetables displayed in crates, some artfully tossed together for color, some separated out by type of vegetable. There are a couple of cracked plastic chairs behind the tables for the helpers to sit. Clyde cultivates a butterfly garden for its beauty and for children to play in when their families stop, but the buildings have an air of practicality. He has a few collected tractors near the highway, one a beautifully painted 1958 Oliver 880 that he restored in memory of his father.

Family continuity and strong ties to the land keep Clyde focused on growing top produce. The 30 acres surrounding the stand are carefully cultivated. "I was born and raised in a brick house right there," Clyde says, pointing up the hill. "These are the fields I ran across."

Clyde has had the stand since 1988. He raises sweet corn, cucumbers, varieties of lettuce in the spring, onions, and spinach. He offers decorative gourds and squash: Dellicato, Carnival, four colors of acorn, sweet dumpling, and Amber Cup butternut squash, all in their season. He offers strawberries, red and black raspberries, blackberries, and will soon get back into growing peaches and apples since canning and preserving is again on the upswing. Then, too, he grows tomatoes. After a friend found a tasty tomato from a produce stand he didn't recognize, Clyde saved the seeds and grew it himself. "The Tasty Toms are all of summertime in one bite," Clyde says. With greenhouses, Clyde extends his tomato season from around June 1 to November. There's a hand-painted phrase on one of Clyde's sheds: Tomato King.

Clyde's brother, Jim "Trapper" Bruckerhoff, works with Clyde and specializes in sweet potatoes. He learned at his grandfather's knee and says, "I got interested in doing it, I started doing it, and I can't quit." He says this with a sort of amused amazement. As he pulls tubers out of the ground, showing off dark red-skinned varieties, white-fleshed ones with orange skin, and even some purplish ones, you can tell he loves the work. He saves seeds each year and grows most of his own plants. Trapper also grows sweet corn, and Clyde remembers their uncle peddling corn out of his Lincoln for 10 cents an ear.

The brothers enjoy the challenge and the benefits of growing vegetables. "Anytime you want to, no matter how bad a day you're having," Clyde says, "you can close your eyes and feel the gentle breeze blow across your face out here. Out here in the dirt, there's absolute honesty. You get everything out of it that you put into it, *and* you can live off of it."

County Line Farm
10334 N. Highway 61
St. Mary, MO 63673

314-994-7204

Vegetable Stand
June through October
Fridays and Saturdays:
8 a.m. - 5 p.m.
Sundays:
Noon - 5 p.m.

Clyde Bruckerhoff (left) and Jim "Trapper" Bruckerhoff

99

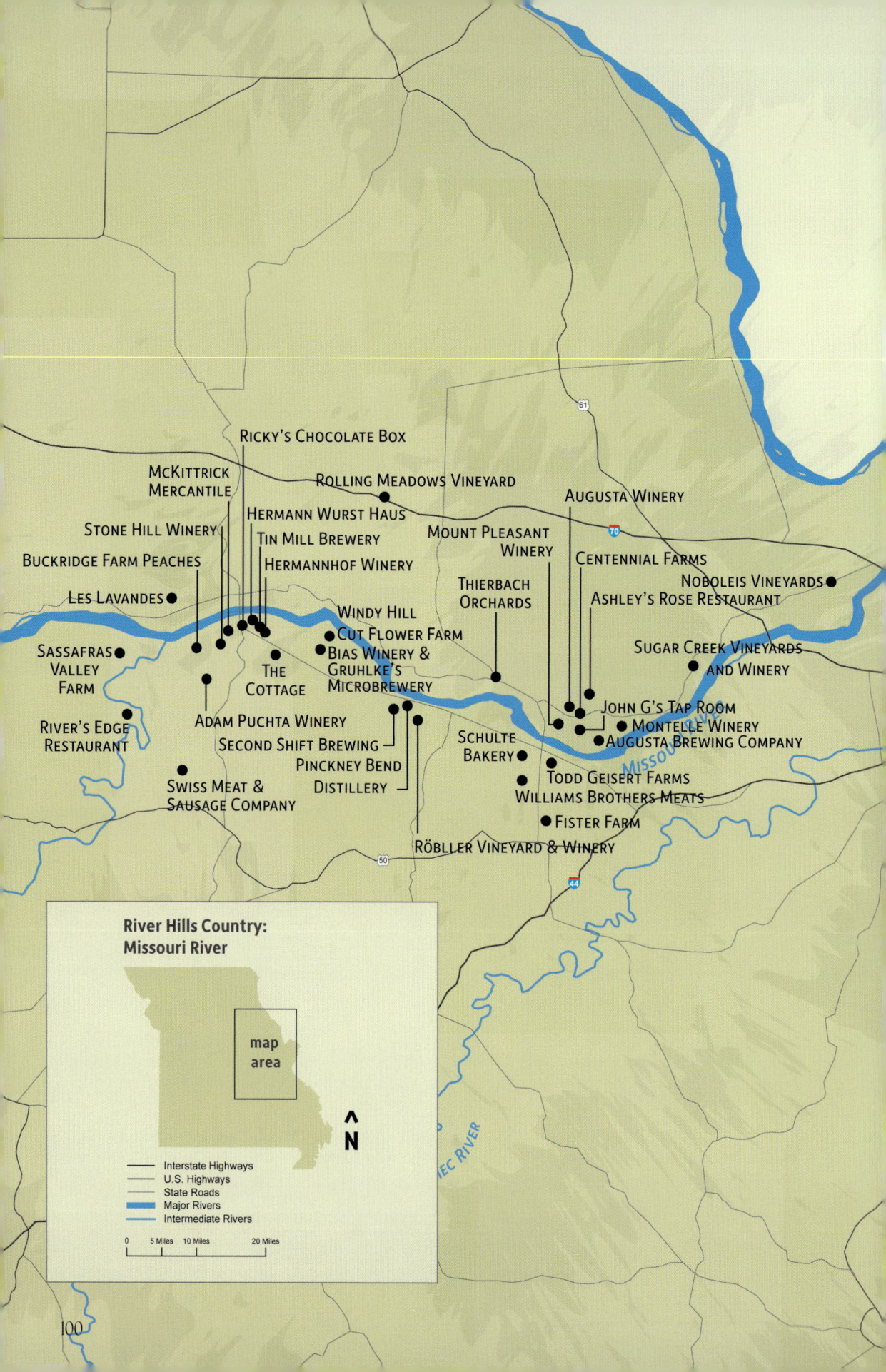

River Hills Country: Missouri River

- Ricky's Chocolate Box
- McKittrick Mercantile
- Rolling Meadows Vineyard
- Augusta Winery
- Stone Hill Winery
- Hermann Wurst Haus
- Tin Mill Brewery
- Mount Pleasant Winery
- Buckridge Farm Peaches
- Hermannhof Winery
- Centennial Farms
- Noboleis Vineyards
- Thierbach Orchards
- Ashley's Rose Restaurant
- Les Lavandes
- Windy Hill Cut Flower Farm
- Sugar Creek Vineyards and Winery
- Sassafras Valley Farm
- The Cottage
- Bias Winery & Gruhlke's Microbrewery
- John G's Tap Room
- River's Edge Restaurant
- Adam Puchta Winery
- Montelle Winery
- Second Shift Brewing
- Augusta Brewing Company
- Schulte Bakery
- Pinckney Bend Distillery
- Todd Geisert Farms
- Swiss Meat & Sausage Company
- Williams Brothers Meats
- Fister Farm
- Röbller Vineyard & Winery

Legend:
- Interstate Highways
- U.S. Highways
- State Roads
- Major Rivers
- Intermediate Rivers

0   5 Miles   10 Miles   20 Miles

N

100

Missouri River Hills

ASHLEY'S ROSE RESTAURANT
AUGUSTA

Home vegetable garden supplies Ashley's Rose Restaurant.

As you drive into the town of Augusta, you'll love the feel of the place, the rolling hills surrounding it, and the businesses that sporadically line the streets. Ashley's Rose Restaurant is located in the heart of town, and Paul Moeser offers Missouri flavors straight from his ample home garden. In fact, he hand picks the tomatoes for his fried tomatoes, and the zucchini, yellow squash, lettuce, radish, green beans, peas, broccoli, and more, staggered throughout the growing season. It's the decor, however, that might draw special interest.

The wall hangings here shift between a Victorian sitting room and the derring-do of early aviation. Fans of flight will note the frame of a Piper Cub hanging from the ceiling and an airplane wing holding glasses and twinkling lights above the bar. "I ran out of room for the full wing span," Paul says, but the uncovered frame of the Piper Cub still conveys the delicate business of flying.

Ashley's Rose often has Wiener schnitzel specials made with pan-fried veal, sweet and sour cabbage, and potato pancakes. The menu offers sandwiches, soups, steaks, ribs, and shrimp. If he has fried tomatoes on offer, the locals say go for it.

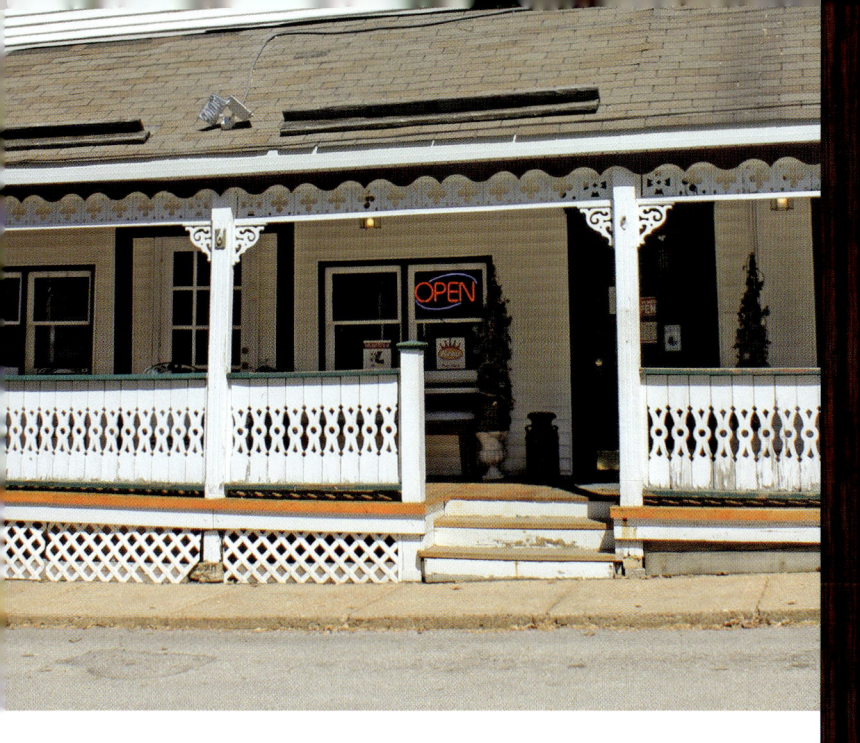

Ashley's Rose Restaurant
5567 Walnut
Augusta, MO 63332

636-482-4108

Sundays:
11 a.m. - 7 p.m.
Tuesdays:
11 a.m - 7 p.m.
Fridays - Saturdays:
11 a.m. - 8:30 p.m

103

AUGUSTA BREWING COMPANY
AUGUSTA

Augusta Brewing Company makes 600 barrels of beer in the middle of wine country.

Nestled in the middle of the Augusta hills, an area known for its wines, Terry and Jeri Heisler serve beer. Augusta Brewing Company produces nearly 600 barrels a year, and with a new expansion in nearby Washington, the Heislers may increase that to 1,800 barrels. Festivals here, such as the Shiver Fest in winter, the October Beer Fest, or the Monster Bike Bash around Halloween, can draw upward of 1,100 people, but some days the atmosphere at the main building, open-sided during warm months, is lower key. Bicyclists from the Katy Trail just steps away, locals, and tourists out for the weekend all stop by, enticed by the lushly wooded land around the seating area and the promise of a handcrafted beer.

Terry and Jeri sit at a table on their terraced hill where bamboo stalks, poppy blooms, and umbrellas welcome visitors. They developed a taste for small-batch brewing while living in Germany in the early years of their marriage, and it inspires their business now. Just across the Missouri River in Washington, the Heislers completed John G's Tap Room in July 2012 in the renovated 1896 Droege grocery building, where Jeri's family first ran a mercantile and then a grocery for 145 years. It now houses brewing operations. Behind the building, overlooking the Missouri River, their already flourishing John G's Bier Deck has its umbrellas unfurled. "We're very rooted in a sense of family and tradition in this region," Jeri says. "We brew beer much the same way they would brew in Germany. When we make sausage at the store (for the catering side of their business), guess what? It's very much like my great-grandfather made it."

They take this interest and care into the brewing house. In fact, the Heisler's brewmaster, Shawn Herrin, won gold with their classic dry Irish stout, named Hyde Park Stout but also called Butch's Stout for Jeri's father, at the 2010 Great American Brew Festival in Denver.

Augusta Brewing Company
5521 Water Street
Augusta, MO 63332

John G's Tap Room
John G's Bier Deck
107 W. Main
Washington, MO 63090

www.augustabrewing.com
636-482-2337

www.johngsbierdeck.com
636-432-1337

April through November
Sundays - Thursdays:
11 a.m. - 7 p.m.
Live music on Sundays

Fridays & Saturdays:
11 a.m. - 9 p.m.
Dinner
5 p.m. - 9 p.m.

December through March
Thursdays - Sundays:
Check website for
abbreviated hours

Wok-Seared Tuna Caesar Salad
Pair with Augusta Witbier or Augusta Blonde Ale; serves 4

For salad:
- 2 tablespoons soy sauce
- 1 tablespoon dark sesame oil
- 1 teaspoon Asian chile sauce (Sriracha)
- 1 tablespoon fresh ginger, finely minced
- 1 pound fresh tuna
- 12 cups lettuce (romaine works best), torn
- 1 red bell pepper, thinly sliced
- 3 ounces enoki mushrooms, pulled apart
- 8 ears baby sweet corn
- 1 cup cooking oil, divided
- 1 cup raw cashews
- ¾ cup fresh Parmesan cheese, grated
- ½ cup cilantro, chopped
- Salt and black pepper, freshly cracked to taste

For dressing:
- 1 cup lemon juice, freshly squeezed
- 1 tablespoon brown sugar
- 1 tablespoon soy sauce
- 1 tablespoon mayonnaise
- ½ cup extra virgin olive oil
- ½ teaspoon Asian chile sauce (Sriracha)
- ½ teaspoon salt
- 2 cloves garlic, minced

In small bowl, combine soy sauce, sesame oil, chile sauce, and ginger. Marinate tuna at least 15 minutes but no more than 8 hours in refrigerator. In large bowl, combine lettuce, bell pepper, mushrooms, and sweet corn. Refrigerate. Combine all ingredients for the salad dressing and set aside. In a pan on medium heat, add ¼ cup oil and cashews and toast until lightly golden. Immediately strain, and then place on paper towel to absorb any excess oil. In a separate pan on medium heat, add enough oil to coat the pan. Allow excess marinade to drip off tuna before adding to the pan. Toast on all sides. The inside should still be red and warm when the tuna is fully cooked. Remove from heat and slice into ¼-inch slices. Arrange tuna slices around salad. Top with cashews, cheese, cilantro, salt, and pepper. Add salad dressing and toss. Serve immediately.

AUGUSTA WINERY
AUGUSTA

Winemaker at Augusta Winery & Montelle Winery hails from a family of California grape growers.

by contributor Nina Bolka, photos by Nina Bolka

Quaint shops and houses line the narrow streets of downtown Augusta. The historic vineyards can be seen sprawling in the distance, highlighting the area's title as the first U.S. Wine District. The rich history, unique soil, and growing potential are what led Tony Kooyumjian here in 1988 to start Augusta Winery.

"I wanted to make the best wine I could," Tony says. "And this was where I could do that."

Tony hails from a family of wine grape growers. His grandmother emigrated from Armenia to San Joaquin Valley, California, in 1915. There, she established and operated a vineyard with the help of her son until 1960. Tony, despite his grape-growing roots, did not originally go into the family business. Instead, he opted for a career in aviation and eventually became a pilot.

While traveling the world, Tony enjoyed wines from different cultures, which reignited his passion for winemaking. Despite not holding a formal degree in enology, he relied on previous experience and studies to return to the field.

"I moved out here in 1988 and purchased the grounds to start Augusta Winery," Tony says. "And from there we have only grown."

Augusta Winery sits at the top of High Street, its bold burgundy awning welcoming visitors. The tasting room has a beautiful bar with complimentary tasting as well as a gift shop. There are also locally produced cheeses and sausages for purchase.

During the warmer months, the winery opens a Wine and Beer Garden, a short walk up the street from the Tasting Room and overlooking downtown Augusta. On weekends, guests can enjoy freshly baked pizzas and wines with live music.

Although the winery is a smaller operation than Tony's other winery, Montelle, he believes the attention poured into every vintage sets them apart. Their wines won the Best Missouri Wine category at the Missouri Governor's Cup in 2004, 2006, and 2007, consistently delivering distinct flavor. Paul Hopen, the vineyard manager, believes Augusta Winery's sustainable practices bring their wines to an elevated level of excellence.

The winery's Norton Reserve, a full-bodied dry red, has a mouth-filling, oak-aged flavor. Its balance and sophistication make it Tony's favorite. There's also the Vignoles, a semi-sweet white, which is perfect for a summer day. With a fruity bouquet and crisp body, it leaves a tingly feeling on the palate and pairs nicely with spicier foods.

The winery produces smaller vintages than neighboring wineries but remains a must-stop destination on the Augusta Wine Trail.

Augusta Winery
5601 High Street
Augusta, MO 63332

www.augustawinery.com
info@augustawinery.com
636-228-4301

Tasting Room
Sundays:
12 p.m. - 6 p.m.
Mondays - Fridays:
10 a.m. - 5:30 p.m.
Saturdays:
10 a.m. - 6 p.m.

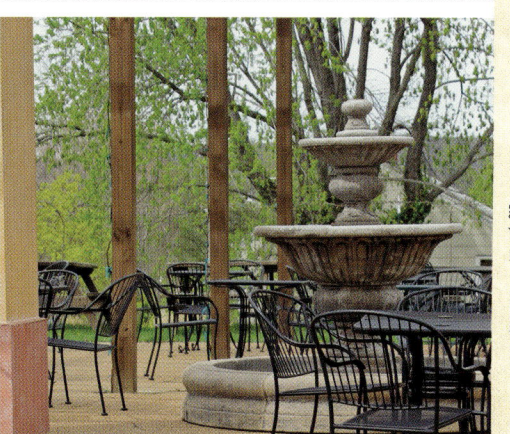

Augusta Winery Filet Mignon with Truffled Mushroom Ragout
Serves 2

3 tablespoons butter
1 garlic clove, chopped
½ teaspoon dried marjoram
12 ounces crimini or button mushrooms, quartered
⅓ cup beef broth
⅓ cup Augusta Norton
3 tablespoons whipping cream
Salt and pepper, to taste
1-½ teaspoons peanut oil
2 (1-inch thick) filet mignons (about 6 ounces each)
½ teaspoon truffle oil

Melt butter in large nonstick skillet over medium heat. Add chopped garlic and marjoram; sauté 30 seconds. Add mushrooms; toss to coat with butter. Sprinkle with salt. Cover and cook until mushrooms have released their juices, about 13 minutes.

Add beef broth, wine, and whipping cream, and bring to a boil. Cook uncovered until mushrooms are tender and sauce coats mushrooms, about 5 minutes. Season mushroom ragout to taste with salt and pepper. (Ragout can be made 3 hours ahead. Cover skillet and refrigerate.)

Heat heavy medium skillet over high heat until hot. Add peanut oil and tilt skillet to coat evenly. Sprinkle steaks with salt and pepper. Add to skillet and cook about 4 minutes per side for medium-rare.

Transfer steaks to plates. Re-warm mushroom ragout in skillet over medium heat, stirring frequently. Spoon ragout partially over steaks and onto plates. Drizzle mushrooms on each plate with truffle oil.

MONTELLE WINERY
AUGUSTA

Enjoy scenic views and fragrant wines at Montelle Winery.

One of the most beautiful views in wine country is from the deck at Montelle Winery near Augusta. The deck, complete with mature trees, captures long views and breezes. Inside, the tasting room offers award-winning wines, food to order, as well as four kinds of brandy made in the winery's distillery: apple, peach, cherry, and grape (grappa).

Owner Tony Kooyumjian of Augusta Winery, which opened in 1988, purchased Montelle Winery in 1998. Clayton Byers founded Montelle Vineyards in 1970 because of the unique Augusta soils and microclimate—the same reasons an eleven square mile area of the Augusta hills was designated as the country's first viticulture area in the United States. These assets, coupled with the sweeping views of the Missouri River Valley are still the draw at Montelle. The wines here win awards, and the foods from Klondike Cafe pair well with the wines. As you sit on the deck, you get a suspended feeling, due in part to the elevation of the deck and the long views and in part to what's in your glass and on your plate. Flavor rules here, but, ah...the view. Come see and taste for yourself.

Montelle Winery Peachy Sangria
Serves 6

1 bottle Montelle Peachy
1-½ cups orange juice
1-¾ cup tonic or club soda
1 cup frozen fruit blend (strawberries, grapes, peaches, honeydew melon, pineapple) or use freshly cut fruit and freeze overnight

Combine wine and orange juice in a pitcher. Refrigerate overnight. When ready to serve, add tonic or soda and frozen fruit. The frozen fruit will keep the drink cool without diluting the flavor.

Montelle Winery
201 Montelle Drive at
Highway 94
Augusta, MO 63332

www.montelle.com
info@montelle.com
636-228-4464

Tasting Room
Daily May through
September
Sundays:
11 a.m. - 6 p.m.
Mondays - Thursdays:
10 a.m. - 5:30 p.m.
Fridays:
10 a.m. - 9 p.m.
Saturdays:
10 a.m. - 10 p.m.

October through April
Sundays:
11 a.m. - 6 p.m.
Mondays-Fridays:
10 a.m. - 5:30 p.m.
Saturdays:
10 a.m. - 6 p.m.

CENTENNIAL FARMS
AUGUSTA

Centennial Farms has grown fruit, vegetables, and herbs for 44 years.

Ellen Knoernschild likes school tours so she can get in her bee suit and tell the students about hives. Bob enjoys the families that come out to let their children pick fruit right from the trees. In all, they've spent more than 44 years operating a fruit, vegetable, and herb farm in Augusta. And that doesn't count the years Bob worked his family farm as a boy.

Centennial Farms in Augusta was a grain and livestock farm in 1854 when Bob's Bavarian grandfather purchased the farm from Leonard Harold. Harold had founded what was to become the town of Augusta on the property in 1821. On the other side of his family, Bob's maternal grandfather was more interested in plants than livestock and operated a vineyard. That vineyard, the Alfred Nahn Winery, actually survived Prohibition when the family switched to making medicinal and communion wine and selling grapes, and one might imagine, keeping their fingers crossed. Between these influences, Bob chose horticulture, met his bride at the University of Missouri in Columbia, and brought her home to the farm. It was 1968, and the Green Movement was stirring. Ellen, raised in St. Louis and new to farming, was intrigued, and their life of peaches, apples, strawberries, blueberries, blackberries, pumpkins, and hayrides began.

Between time as teachers in nearby Washington and Ellen's accounting work in St. Louis, the couple also made the taste of summer last with their commercial kitchen on the property. Ellen cooks apple butter in a copper kettle with an automatic stirrer, which is better than "standing outside with a paddle stirring over burning wood," she says. Her apple butter, strawberry preserves, honey, blackberry syrup, and more are in demand at the farmers' markets they attend and at special festivals such as Kimmswick's Strawberry Festival, for which Ellen makes more than 38 cases of strawberry preserves.

The farm produces seasonal vegetables, too: squash, tomatoes, peppers, eggplant, and broccoli. The Knoernschild Centennial Farms shop is in the barn, rafters, peck baskets, wood tables, bins, and all. With 24 varieties of apples and pumpkins in the fall, 20 types of preserves, and more, it's a place you'll want to see for yourself, and walk away with armfuls.

Centennial Farms
199 Jackson Street
Augusta, MO 63332

www.centennialfarms.biz
636-228-4338

Farm
July and August
Thursdays - Sundays:
Noon - 5 p.m.

Daily September and October
10 a.m. - 5 p.m.

Market
July through early November

Tower Grove Farmers' Market
Saturdays

Maplewood Farmers' Market
Wednesdays

Contributor to Fair Shares CSA

Traditional Blackberry Cobbler
Serves 4

- 1 quart blackberries
- 2 tablespoons cornstarch
- 1-⅓ cup sugar
- 4 refrigerated biscuits or ½ standard biscuit recipe

Preheat oven to 400°F. Grease a 9x9-inch baking pan and set aside. Mix the cornstarch and sugar and add to the blackberries. Heat to boiling in a medium saucepan or in a microwave oven. Pour into baking pan and top with unbaked biscuits. Bake until biscuits are brown on top. Serve hot with ice cream or whipped cream.

MOUNT PLEASANT WINERY
AUGUSTA

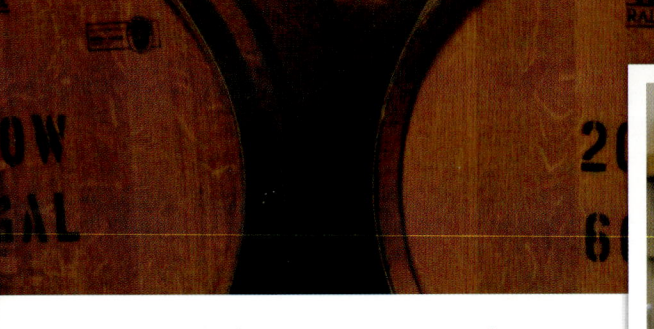

Mount Pleasant Winery produces 31 wines from 12 grape varieties.

by contributor Nina Bolka, photos by Nina Bolka

Mount Pleasant Winery is the oldest and largest producer of grapes in the Augusta region, growing more than 12 varieties on 78 acres. The winery's expansive landscape overlooks the Missouri River Valley, where George and Frederick Muench, two brothers from Germany, established Mount Pleasant in 1859.

"These cellars were originally built in 1881," Chuck Dressel, the current owner and president of Mount Pleasant, says. "And today we're still using them."

Dressel appreciates the rich history of his winery and believes in sharing it. Every weekend from April to October, guests can take a complimentary tour and see the cellars, which the Muench brothers crafted from natural materials found in the Augusta area. When Prohibition laws were implemented in 1920, the entirety of Mount Pleasant's vineyards were destroyed. It was not until 1966 that Lucian and Eva Dressel purchased the former vineyard and replanted. By 1980, Augusta was declared the first wine district in the United States.

Chuck purchased the winery from his uncle Lucian in 1992 and has been growing ever since.

The grounds are expansive, as are the tasting room and gift shop. Here, guests can pay $5 for five generous samples, then wander outside to view the rolling vineyards. The Appellation Cafe, which serves lunch every weekend from April to October, has a large patio for diners but transforms at night for different events.

"We put on a lot of concerts and events," Chuck says. "Last year we also had around 250 weddings."

Despite the busy nature of Mount Pleasant, they continue to craft award-winning wines every year. Winemaker Colin Pennington oversees the sustainable practices and produces more than 31 wines. Their 2010 Norton Missouri, a deep red wine with blueberry notes, won the Midwest Wine Challenge for the Best Norton. They have also received high marks for their Cabernet Sauvignon American NV, a delicate and jammy Cabernet with a toasty finish.

"People told me I couldn't grow a cabernet in Missouri, so I proved them wrong," Chuck says.

He admits he is partial towards his Cabernet but still enjoys many other Mount Pleasant wines. Considering more than 60,000 vines are grown at Mount Pleasant, there's a lot of range in flavors. This, Chuck believes, makes operating a larger winery fun.

"We have something for everyone," he says. This, plus the long views of the Missouri River Valley, makes Mount Pleasant a great place to get away from the city for the day.

Mount Pleasant Winery
5634 High Street
Augusta, MO 63332

www.mountpleasant.com
info@mountpleasant.com
636-482-9463

April through October
Mondays - Fridays:
11 a.m. - 5 p.m.
Saturdays - Sundays:
11 a.m. - 5:30 p.m.

Daily November
through March
Noon - 4 p.m.

Mushroom Bordeaux Sauce

3 tablespoons butter
3 tablespoons flour
½ cup baby bella mushrooms, chopped
½ cup roasted shallots, chopped
1 teaspoon rosemary, chopped
1 teaspoon thyme, chopped
1 cup Mount Pleasant Cabernet Sauvignon
½ cup beef stock
Salt and cracked pepper

Melt the butter in a small sauce pan. Whisk in the flour to make a roux. Stir in the mushrooms, shallots, rosemary, and thyme. Cook for about 5 minutes. Slowly pour the Cabernet into the pan while whisking. Cook wine down to about half the amount. This will cook out the alcohol and give the sauce a richer flavor. Then add the beef stock until you get the sauce consistency you want. Add salt and cracked pepper to taste.

Serving suggestion: Mushroom Bordeaux sauce is great over a strip steak with blue cheese crumbles on top.

113

NOBOLEIS VINEYARDS
AUGUSTA

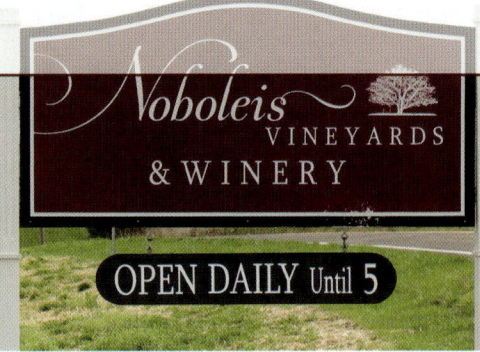

Noboleis Vineyards hosts live music on the vineyard hilltop.
by contributor Nina Bolka, photos by Nina Bolka

A large mulberry tree situated on a hilltop overlooks Noboleis Vineyards, creating a perfect viewing point for visitors to enjoy wine on a warm summer day. Manager and family member Chris Newbold stands beneath the elaborate branches, which swing back and forth in the Augusta wind.

"This tree has been through a lot," she says, citing a tornado that ripped through the vineyard's property in February of 2011. "But it's still standing strong."

The Nolan family, as collective owners of Noboleis Vineyards, emulates this mulberry tree's perseverance. Robert Nolan, Chris's father, traveled to the West Coast in 2003 and uncovered his passion for the wine industry. Soon enough, he and his wife, Lou Ann, pursued his dream to go into the wine business and purchased ground along Augusta's Wine Trail in 2004.

Noboleis Vineyards has flourished since then thanks to collaborative family efforts, which are embedded in the vineyard's name. Lou Ann combined both of her daughters' married surnames, Newbold and Geis, with Nolan, serendipitously crafting "Noboleis."

"A lot of people ask us if it's a French name," Chris jokes. "I think we got pretty lucky with how it came out."

Brandon Dixon, the current winemaker and general manager, joined the Noboleis family in 2009 for the first harvest. Brandon has worked in Augusta more than six years and learned the art of winemaking from his uncle, who used to work at another winery in Augusta.

"I wanted to make a wine that I would enjoy, and others would as well," Brandon says. "Here I've been able to craft for different palates."

The winery's variety of flavors did not go unnoticed at the 2010 Missouri Governor's Cup, when many of their first vintage wines took home medals. Suddenly, Noboleis Vineyards gained recognition despite being the newest estate vineyard and winery in the Augusta region. In 2012, Noboleis Vineyards received a Gold Medal for their Steepleview and a Best-in-Class Award for their Traminette.

The family expanded upon the property, opening a tasting room in October of 2010, which is shaded by the grand mulberry tree. Here, visitors walk in and can enjoy a free tasting or purchase food from the cafe. In the winter, the cafe offers soup and pasta dishes but switches to a lighter menu by spring.

At the end of April, we start to get really busy," Chris says. "And that's when we put up the tents outside on the hilltop so guests can enjoy wine outside with live music. Bands come out on weekends so all ages can enjoy themselves. Brandon believes that creating a family-centered atmosphere is not only important to them, but also to their guests.

Of course, the wines are the star attraction at Noboleis Vineyards. From their best-selling Steepleview, an off dry red, to a fruity Traminette, there is something for everyone.

Winemaker Brandon Dixon and co-owner Chris Newbold

Noboleis Vineyards
100 Hemsath Road
Augusta, MO 63332

www.noboleisvineyards.com
info@noboleisvineyards.com
636-482-4500

Tasting Room
Sundays:
Noon - 5 p.m.
Mondays - Fridays:
11 a.m. - 5 p.m.
Saturdays:
11 a.m. - 5 p.m.

Noboleis Wild Mushroom Pasta Sauce
Serves 4 with pasta

1 cup vegetable broth
1-½ ounces dried wild mushrooms (bolete or porcini)
1 cup Noboleis Chambourcin
2 tablespoons butter, divided
24 ounces portobello mushrooms, washed and chopped
4 large shallots, minced

4 large garlic cloves, minced
2 tablespoons sage, chopped
3 tablespoons flour
½ cup parsley, chopped
Salt and black pepper, freshly ground to taste
Pasta of choice
Parmesan

Bring the broth to a boil. Put the dried mushrooms into a glass bowl and pour the boiling broth over them. Let them steep in the broth for 20 minutes. Drain the mushrooms, reserving the broth. Mix the drained broth with the Noboleis Chambourcin.

Next, heat a tablespoon of butter in a large skillet over medium-high heat. Add the chopped portobello mushrooms and let sit, without stirring for about 4 minutes, or until they have thoroughly browned on one side. Stir and let them cook on the other side, again without stirring for about 4 minutes. Add the shallots, garlic, sage, and steeped wild mushrooms. Turn the heat to low and cook until they are fragrant and soft. Add the second tablespoon of butter and when melted, add the flour. Whisk rapidly letting the flour thicken with the butter into a paste.

Slowly add the broth and Chambourcin mixture while whisking rapidly. Cook over medium-low heat and continue whisking until the mixture thickens. Add the chopped parsley and stir until wilted. Season with salt and pepper to taste. Serve immediately over your favorite pasta and top with fresh Parmesan. We serve this over our homemade butternut squash ravioli.

115

BIAS WINERY
BERGER

Bias Winery & Gruhlke's Microbrewery was the second winery-microbrewery combination in the country.

Kirk and Carol Grass loved coming out to Bias Winery in Berger on weekends to relax with friends over wine. Jim and Norma Bias, the original owners of Bias Winery, sold wines out of what is the office now. It was a local getaway. Jim added on, and the winery started to grow. "We lived in New Haven," Carol says, "and always liked the tranquility of getting off the beaten path. It was a Sunday ritual."

The winery sits on the hills overlooking the river bottoms near Berger, literally off the beaten path, and it fit that need to get away from daily cares. Carol, who worked in health care, and Kirk, a high school teacher, liked it so much they took over the winery in 2004.

Today, Kirk and Carol grow Catawba, Chambourcin, DeChaunac, Seyval, Vidal, Fredonia, and other varieties on their 67 acres. Their wine production capacity is 9,000 gallons a year, and their focus is on the customers. "It's one customer at a time," Kirk says, "We make it, bottle it, sell it, and get to see the reaction right up front." The winery offers a broad variety of wines, from dry, red Norton, Chambourcin, and DeChaunac, to sweet raspberry, apple, and strawberry Weisser Flieders. Kirk and Carol like doing events, and weekends are filled with adult Easter egg hunts, nature trail scavenger hunts, barbecue and chili cook-offs, croquet tournaments, Wine Trail events, and more.

Though nearly 70 percent of their business comes from out-of-town visitors, Carol and Kirk measure their success by the locals. "We knew if we were doing things right, the locals would still come out for their own Sunday ritual, like we used to do," Carol says. The whole point for Carol and Kirk is to create a special place, where people can come out to relax, leave their cares behind, and return home with a feeling of having been genuinely welcomed.

GRUHLKE'S MICROBREWERY
BERGER

On the same property, Kirk and Carol offer craft beers, and in 1998, it was the first microbrewery-winery combination in Missouri and the second in the nation. Kirk and Carol inherited some recipes, developed more, and now produce 500 gallons a year in 10-gallon batches using 30 recipes. Seven microbrews are typically on tap at any one time. In late summer, there might be Missouri Wheat, a light-bodied wheat malt beer; Done Did It Dortmunder, a dark gold and mildly caramel beer; Chubby Stout, a dark Irish ale; Nate's Belgian Tripel with its golden color and mild, spicy character; Black Lager, a smooth European-style lager with balanced roasted flavors and moderate bitterness from the hops; Naughty's Ale, a clean, crisp India Pale Ale; Gruhlke's Light; and Opa Willy's Homemade Rootbeer. Sampler platters mean you don't have to choose. Knowing how wine works really helped when making craft beers, Kirk says, and seasonal offerings make the tastes innovative.

Beer Marinade

¼ cup Gruhlke's Wheat beer
½ cup Italian salad dressing
1-2 tablespoons Worcestershire sauce

Mix all ingredients. Marinate meat for a minimum of two hours, but it's best marinated overnight. Reserve part of the marinade to baste while grilling.

Chilled Berry Soup
Serves 2

1 quart fresh strawberries, stemmed
⅓ cup Strawberry Weisser Flieder Wine
¼ cup milk (optionally use half-and-half to make soup richer)
⅓ cup sugar
1 tablespoon lemon juice
1 teaspoon vanilla extract
1 cup sour cream

Place strawberries in a food processor; cover and process until pureed. Add the wine, milk, sugar, lemon juice, and vanilla; cover and process until blended. Pour into a large bowl; whisk in the sour cream until smooth. Cover and refrigerate until soup is thoroughly chilled, about two hours.

Bias Winery & Gruhlke's Brewery
3166 Highway B
Berger, MO 63014

www.biaswinery.com
bias@fidnet.com
573-834-5475

April through October
Mondays - Fridays:
10 a.m. - 5 p.m.
Saturdays:
10 a.m. - 6 p.m.
Sundays:
11 a.m. - 6 p.m.

November through March
Mondays - Sundays:
11 a.m. - 5 p.m.

Festival Weekends
Fridays - Sundays:
Until 6 p.m.

Applesauce Glaze for Grilled Pork

1 cup applesauce
¼ cup Apple Weisser Flieder
Pork tenderloins

Mix well and brush over pork tenderloins during the last 10 minutes of grilling.

WINDY HILL CUT FLOWER FARM
BERGER

**Windy Hill Cut Flower Farm
has winding paths, shady gardens, and wildflowers.**

Mary Fritz's Windy Hill Cut Flower Farm has the charm you might expect of a farm devoted to flowers. The driveway has a shady garden with winding paths alongside it, and the homestead is a beautifully renovated 1854 walnut log house with original red pine floors and an exposed log wall in the kitchen. Mary and her husband, Dr. Robert Fritz, renovated the original log barn and a potting shed that used to be a smokehouse. The farm views are soothing and rolling. But it's Mary and her flowers that leave a lasting impression. This woman knows plants and what is pleasing to the eye.

"When I learned landscape design, I learned how to look at textures, depth, to look with a different perspective," Mary says. This perspective creates spectacular flowers for weddings, restaurants, and other floral customers. "It's to the point that I drive along the road, and when other people see houses, I see plants. It's your mind's eye." She sees flower arranging as landscaping on a small scale.

And it shows. Mary's arrangements blend classic bouquet flowers with a sophisticated use of wildflowers. For a bridal customer, Mary will get the bride's colors and date of the ceremony and explain the range of flowers and the colors that are blooming at that time. "They're brave girls," Mary says, as she fans out photos of eclectic mixes of berries, herbs, and sometimes what grows along fence rows.

Windy Hill has 48 acres of wildflowers on rolling hills and some woody copses that Mary checks for nature's bounty. If you go with Mary as she walks or drives her Gator through a field, you notice new textures yourself and begin to see Mary's world of unbounded, free-flowing floral design. "There," she says, pointing to tufts of plants sprouting in the field, "there's Slender Mint."

Some plants she picks are classics used in unusual ways. She points out limelight hydrangea, fennel, mums, and viburnum tips and leaves, or hosta leaves that she might use to wrap the base of an arrangement, or honeysuckle to tie groupings of flowers together. Sometimes black pearl peppers are a good contrast, she says, with white flowers. One bride's bouquet sported Queen Anne's Lace, dill, navy Solomon Seal, white Asiatic lily, purple ironweed, white fever few, and a little touch of lily of the valley leaf. "I like the way it peeks out," Mary explains. A boutonnière might be made from sage with rosemary with a bit of purple ironweed. A centerpiece has dangling green berries and sweet autumn clematis that curls around, creating more texture. "I like to use hops, foxtail," Mary says.

Mary learned her love of flowers from her grandmother and mother, who were incredible gardeners, and from German Four Square Gardening, a forerunner to today's organic growing techniques. She has a horticulture degree from St. Louis Community College at Meramec as well as a bachelor's degree from Western Illinois University, but she earned her stripes in the field while sporting poison ivy outbreaks. When she and Robert were clearing the original homestead of it's overgrown brambles in 1990, they both were covered. "We had his and her brush hogs, tractors, and chain saws," she says, "and there were trunks of poison ivy on the barn."

Mary's business started by people calling for flowers for their events, then a bride called, and soon, Mary was working full time. She has college students who are interested in horticulture, and Missouri's heritage plants help out. She has a working five-year calendar of when plants bloom. She knows her land and her plants. Her only regret is timing. "I wish I'd started doing this when I was younger."

**Windy Hill
Cut Flower Farm**
4103 Highway Z
Berger, MO 63014

wndhl@fidnet.com
573-834-5560

By appointment only

Windy Hill's Herbes de Provence Rub for Meat

2 tablespoons dried oregano
2 tablespoons dried thyme
1 tablespoon dried rosemary
1 tablespoon fennel seeds
1-½ teaspoon dried rubbed sage

Mix all herbs together and use as a rub on lamb, chicken, pork roast, or sprinkle as extra seasoning over pizza. This rub is especially good on grilled vegetables.

SUGAR CREEK VINEYARDS AND WINERY
DEFIANCE

An Italian grandfather selecting wines for Sunday dinner planted the idea for Sugar Creek Vineyards and Winery.

Becky and Ken Miller left their Kirkwood home and working life to start Sugar Creek Winery in Defiance in 1994. "It was mid-life madness," Becky says. But the pull of the vines stemmed from Ken's childhood memories of his Italian grandfather, Michael Belmonte, bringing wines up from his cellar for Sunday dinners in Chicago. That interest transferred to Ken and eventually to the hillside of Sugar Creek. The effect is a welcoming, friendly spot, an almost-bluff, overlooking the Missouri River valley within easy driving distance of St. Louis.

Soon after opening, son Chris Lorch began making the wines, and they have developed a fine array: Vidal Blanc, Chardonel, Chambourcin, Cynthiana, and Michael's Signature Red, all estate wines and others such as Birdlegs Blush, named for Becky, as well as port. Chris developed his wine skills after trying beer brewing first and then working at a California winery for two years. "I focus on the vineyards," he says, and tends each vine around 10 times a year for pruning, tying, and other processes before harvest. "If you start with a good base, you end up where you want." The care put into the land and grapes is obvious when you look around at the well-manicured land surrounding the winery building. Visitors can sit on the front deck, patio, or grounds and look out over a long vista of trees and rolling hills.

With 14 wine varieties now offered, Chris has a difficult time selecting a favorite. "It changes with the day, the company, the weather and the other flavors I'm experiencing." He experiments with port in recipes, and you can sense his attention to detail and flavor nuance when he describes flavor combinations.

Chris Lorch and Becky Miller

Morel Mushrooms with Port
Serves 4

1 pound morel mushrooms
⅓ stick salted butter
4 to 8 ounces Sugar Creek Port
Dash ground cinnamon
1 tablespoon brown sugar

In a large pan over medium heat, sauté mushrooms in the butter until they begin to shrink. Add port in small increments, stirring gently between. Let port reduce to about two-thirds or one-half of its volume. Add cinnamon to taste and brown sugar.

Sugar Creek Vineyards and Winery
125 Boone Country Lane
Defiance, MO 63341

www.sugarcreekwines.com
636-987-2400

Sundays:
Noon - 5:30 p.m.
Mondays - Saturdays:
10 a.m. - 5:30 p.m.
Fridays in June, July, August:
10 a.m. - Dusk

Port Marinade for Pork

4 pork chops
1-1/8 cup Sugar Creek Port
2 dashes black pepper
1/4-1/2 cup olive oil
Dash cayenne pepper
1 teaspoon ground cumin
Dash cinnamon
Black pepper to taste
Ground cumin to taste
1/2 cup apple butter or applesauce

With a sharp knife, poke holes in the pork. In a deep dish or pan, mix all the remaining ingredients. Place pork chops in the marinade and let sit for 3 to 4 hours, turning once or twice. Prepare grill. Grill meat 2 minutes on high on one side, turn pork chops and cook other side on high for 2 minutes. Reduce heat to low. Baste meat with marinade. Continue to cook for another 4 to 5 minutes. Turn, baste again, and cook on low for 4 to 5 minutes until done.

Variation: Marinate chicken and grill.

123

ADAM PUCHTA WINERY
HERMANN

Adam Puchta Winery dates back to before Prohibition.

Tim Puchta has a laugh that welcomes anyone stepping through the doors of the Adam Puchta Winery in Hermann. In fact, the entire winery has a warm, inviting feel. The land is rolling and gorgeous on the hillside where Norton grapes are growing, and the Puchta wines are lovely on the tongue.

Six generations ago, the Puchta family established the winery in 1855, and then two generations later lost everything in Prohibition. That story still seems close enough to touch to Tim, whose grandfather had to watch as his labor and family resources drained away, as casks were smashed and vineyards torn out. Of the 10 or more large early 1900s wooden wine casks in the Puchta wine cellar, one remains. Though that generation of Puchta's replanted their land in other crops, in 1989 Tim and his father, Randolph, began again. Now Adam Puchta's vineyards are re-emerging as one of Missouri's winery gems.

Fourteen types of wine and two ports and a sherry are on offer for visitors to taste. The winery, known for its smooth-on-the-tongue wines, might make dry wine drinkers interested in sweet or semi-sweet. And those that eschew dry wines might nod approval after a sip of one of the winery's Nortons.

Tim, the sixth generation to work the land two miles outside of Hermann, uses his grandmother's old rock-walled summer kitchen, where she baked and cooked on a woodstove, as the wine shop, housing wine gifts and bottles of wine to buy. Adam Puchta Winery is a wonderful stop for the story of Missouri wine, as well as for tasty sips.

Puchtarita

Take a bar pitcher full of ice and pour one bottle of Adam Puchta Vignoles into it. Add 2 shots of Grand Marnier and liquid tequila mix of your choice (without the tequila) to taste. Now you have a refreshing end-of-summer wine margarita.

Adam Puchta Winery
1947 Frene Creek Road
Hermann, MO 65041

www.adampuchtawine.com
info@adampuchtawine.com
573-486-5596

Summer
Sundays:
11 a.m. - 6 p.m.
Mondays - Saturdays:
9 a.m. - 6 p.m.

Winter
Sundays:
11 a.m. - 5 p.m.
Mondays - Saturdays:
9 a.m. - 5 p.m.

Boeuf Bourguignon

3 pounds beef blade or chuck steak
3 cups Adam Puchta Hunter's Red wine
3 garlic cloves, crushed
Dried parsley, to taste
Dried thyme, to taste
Dried celery, to taste
Dried bay leaves, to taste

6 tablespoons butter, divided
1 onion, chopped
½ (16-ounce) bag of baby carrots, sliced in half
2 tablespoons all purpose flour
8 ounces bacon, cut in small strips
12 ounces shallots, peeled and left whole
8 ounces small button mushrooms

Trim away any excess fat on the meat and cut into 1-inch cubes. Place the meat, Hunter's Red, and garlic in a large bowl and season with dried parsley, thyme, celery, and bay leaves to taste. Cover with plastic wrap and refrigerate overnight.

Preheat oven to 300°F. Next, drain the meat, setting the marinade aside. Add 2 tablespoons of the butter, the onions and carrots to a large pan and cook over low heat for 10 minutes, stirring occasionally. Remove from the heat. Add 2 tablespoons of the butter to a large frying pan on high heat and, in small batches, brown the meat. Set browned meat aside with the vegetables. Pour the leftover marinade into the frying pan and boil for about 30 seconds, deglazing the pan. Remove from the heat and set aside. Sprinkle the meat and vegetables with the flour, stirring constantly until the mixture is well coated with flour. Pour in the reserve marinade, move the meat and vegetables pan to the stove and bring to a boil, stirring well. Continue to stir the mixture well while boiling for about 30 seconds, and cover and place in the oven for about 2 hours.

Heat the remaining butter in a clean frying pan, cooking the bacon and shallots for 8 to 10 minutes until softened. Add the mushrooms and cook for about 3 minutes until browned. Drain and add the shallots, mushrooms, and bacon to the casserole. Cover and return to the oven for 30 minutes. Skim any fat off the surface and season to taste prior to serving.

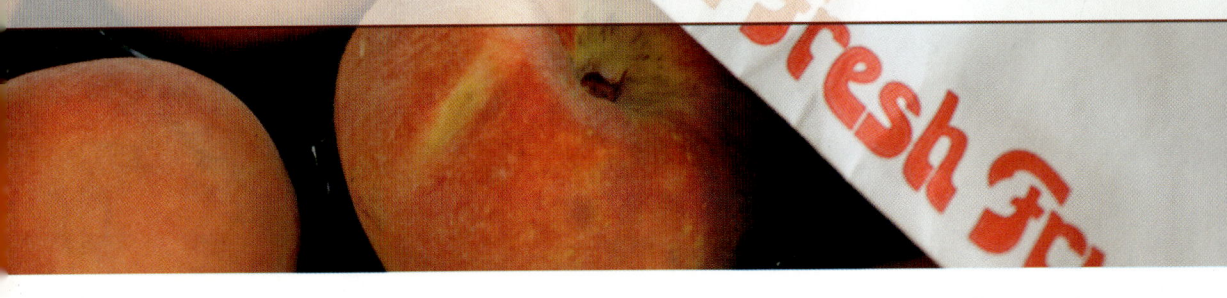

BUCKRIDGE FARM PEACHES
HERMANN

Sold from a truck, Buckridge Peaches are some of the best in the state.

photography by contributor Nathan Furstenau

Buckridge Farm sits atop a spectacular Missouri hill, and the breezes running through the trees there carry ripe fruit aromas and the sound of rustling leaves. The warm and earthy scent on top of that ridge makes it possible to visualize it as it had been years ago: a vineyard, one of Hermann's many before Prohibition. Now, the peach trees Larry Bock and Tim Wright planted in 2000 produce some of the best peaches in the state, due to lush soil and good tending. Most mornings in midsummer, Larry and Tim are picking peaches by 6 a.m. You can find those fresh-picked gems starting at 8 a.m. at the Hermann Lumber parking lot, 603 Market Street in Hermann, every summer from early July to mid-August. Larry and Tim's Red Haven peaches are the first to ripen, and starting around July 12, the Buckridge varieties come like seven-day overlapping waves. After Red Haven, Saturn comes next, then Ernie's Choice, Glo Haven, Contender, and Summer Pearl varieties.

At the Buckridge truck, the customers that come in a steady stream know those peach names. Tim and Larry are bagging fruit, talking about the variety in season that week, and picking out single peaches to fill bags. Tim eyes a good one, turns it quickly in his palm, and then places it gently on top of the others for a customer.

"A man from Georgia came by once," Larry says, "and didn't believe we'd have as good a peach as he was used to back home. I told him he'd better bite into it leaning out." Both Tim and Larry chuckle as they remember the fresh peach juice dripping down the man's chin.

Larry and Ruth Bock and Tim and Joyce Wright are partners in the peach farm, and the men have been friends since they worked in a bakery together in their teens. Something works well in that partnership; you can tell from their mutual knowledge and excitement about peach varieties. Their orchard, on perhaps the most perfect spot to grow peaches in the area, produces about 500 to 600 bushels a year. Most of those, up to as many as 2,800 peaches on a Saturday, sell by the quarter-peck, half-peck, and full peck bags right off the truck at the lumberyard parking lot. The rest go to groceries in Hermann and Jefferson City.

In 2006, the men added elderberries to their farm. Larry and Tim planted a one-acre plot of elderberries, or 900 plants, and Tim added five more acres in 2010. The elderberry packs a punch of antioxidants as well as vitamins A, B, and C and has long been used in herbal teas for ailments such as respiratory problems, colds, and the flu. The elderberry is hardy, Tim says, and grows well in Missouri. Tim and Larry are part of the River Hills Elderberry Producers group, which collects wild and cultivated berries from growers around the state, processes them into juices and jam, and sells the products.

Buckridge Farm Peaches
1773 Buckridge Lane
Hermann, MO 65041

573-486-5767

Hermann Lumber Parking Lot
603 Market Street
Early July through Mid-August
Mondays - Saturdays:
8 a.m. until sold out

Tim Wright (left) and Larry Bock

Everyday Peach Cobbler
Serves 6

Filling:
5-6 peaches, peeled and sliced
½ cup sugar
3 tablespoons butter, in pieces
Dash salt

Batter:
1 cup flour
1 cup sugar
1 teaspoon baking powder
1 egg, beaten
6 tablespoons water
1 teaspoon vanilla

Preheat your oven to 350°F. Lightly coat an 11x7-inch baking dish with nonstick oil spray, butter, or shortening. Place the sliced peaches into the dish and sprinkle with sugar and a dash of salt. Dot with butter. For the batter, mix the flour, sugar, and baking powder. Add the beaten egg, water, and vanilla. Stir to blend. Spoon the batter over the peaches. Do not stir. Bake about 45 minutes or light brown. Best when served with ice cream.

HERMANNHOF WINERY
HERMANN

Hermannhof Winery has its own shops, guest rooms, and cottages.

Paul LeRoy, general manager and winemaker for Hermannhof Winery in Hermann, tended and sanitized tanks, barrels, hoses, and presses when he first started there as a cellar hand in high school. After 31-plus years, he still values elbow grease and timing, now as winemaker and general manager. He values the fruit most of all. "If you're serious in the wine business, you have to be serious in the vineyard."

When the wine is right, LeRoy says, everything is in balance: "Good clean fruit and good clean fermentation," is the key. LeRoy, who credits expert advice along the way, has amassed years of knowledge by closely watching the vines, plus, he says, monitoring "whatever Mother Nature throws at you. Wines and juices don't have a calendar."

Jim and Mary Dierberg purchased the cellars in 1974, but the history of the property is deep in the story of Hermann. Hermannhof's 10 stone cellars and brick tasting room are on the National Register of Historic Places and are among the early structures in Hermann. They were built in 1852 to produce beer as well as wine. By 1904, the area produced upward of three million gallons of wine per year until Prohibition shuttered almost all wine activity. Today, Hermannhof has 32 acres in grape vines and produces about 15,000 cases or 36,000 gallons of wine per year. The wines are sold at their multiple shops in St. Louis, Kansas City, Columbia, and Jefferson City.

In addition to wine tasting, Hermannhof offers guest rooms and stone hillside cottages that were moved onto the property from the surrounding countryside. Many of the cottages belonged to small vintners who grew their own grapes and made wine in their homes, earning them the label "house wineries." The setting is ideal for looking out over the vista of the Missouri River as well as historic Hermann.

Hermannhof Winery
330 E. First Street
Hermann, MO 65041

www.hermannhof.com
800-393-0100

Mondays - Saturdays:
10 a.m. - 5 p.m.
Sundays:
11 a.m. - 5 p.m.

129

JANET HURST CHEESE-MAKING CLASSES
HERMANN

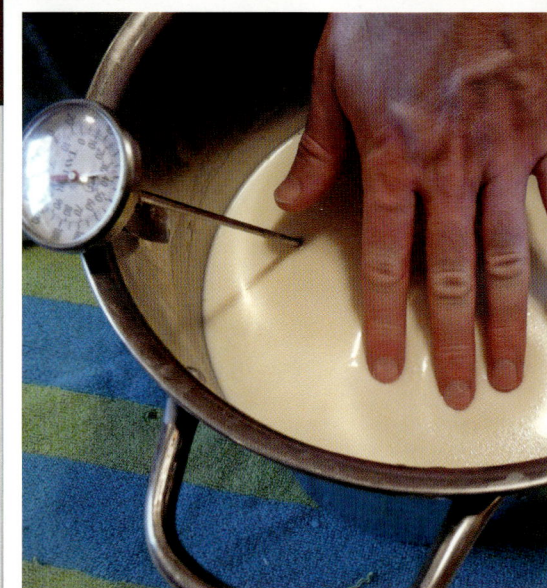

Learn to make cheese with Janet Hurst.

Janet Hurst says she is not responsible for anyone running out to buy a goat once they take a cheese class from her. It just happens.

Janet, who lives in the Hermann area, demystifies cheese making, and in one of her afternoon classes, you can learn to make chevre, mozzarella, ricotta, or even aged cheeses such as cheddar and Brie. In her introductory class, she discusses curds and whey, the aging process, and more importantly, she guides students as they make and taste really good cheese.

"One of the things I like about cheese is that it does capture the essence of a region," she says. "It combines science and art and regional flavor."

In the Hermann area, she teaches classes on kochkaese cheese. "Every time I teach a class, someone will tell me, my grandmother would make this cheese, put it in a pillowcase and hang it to dry on the clothesline." The process was part of the kitchen history of the settlers of the area and links current residents to that past.

And for Janet, the goats capture your heart. "I was always interested in the back-to-the-land movement. My grandmother produced her own foods and I wanted to do that for my family," Janet says of her beginning days as a cheese maker. After she got her first goat, she was hooked. "That goat really stole my heart," she says. Eventually, she went on to have 40 goats. She worked in a creamery in Kirksville and helped in the goat dairy and "the world opened up." She went on to study cheese making in Canada, Vermont, and Israel. "I liked small artisan-style cheese making and I wanted to teach others to do the same."

If you have a group, call ahead for a special class. Or, join an already scheduled class by Janet. It will tickle your tastebuds.

Janet Hurst
Cheese-Making Classes

www.cheesewriter.com
jlynnehurst@yahoo.com
660-216-1749

Fresh Chevre
Serves 12-18

1 gallon of fresh goat milk, pasteurized (instructions below)
2 drops of liquid rennet* dissolved in ¼ cup non-chlorinated water
½ to 1 teaspoon non-iodized salt to taste
⅛ teaspoon cheese culture (Mesophilic DVI MA)*

*Rennet and cheese culture are available through cheese-making supply houses

Equipment Needed:
Heavy cooking pot, large enough to hold 1 gallon of milk
Dairy thermometer
Ladle
Slotted spoon
String
Flour sack dish towel
Colander

Pour the goat milk into the cooking pot. Heat the milk slowly to 86°F. At 86°F, remove the pot from heat.
Sprinkle the culture over the top of the milk and gently stir, making sure the culture is dissolved and well integrated into the milk. Allow this mixture to sit for about 45 minutes, so the culture has time to develop.
Add the rennet mixed in water and stir, coming up from the bottom of the pot, until the culture and rennet are mixed thoroughly into the milk. Stir gently for about 1 minute. Let the mixture rest, covered with a cloth, in a warm place (70°F) for 12 to 18 hours. The gel will thicken to the consistency of yogurt while it is resting.
When the gel has thickened, it is time to ladle the mass into a colander lined with a flour sack tea towel. Place the colander in the sink or over a large bowl. With a slotted spoon, gently transfer the gel mass, called the curd, into the lined colander. Keep ladling until all the curd is in the colander. The leftover liquid is called whey, which can be used to make bread or discarded as a waste product. Once all the curd is in the colander, gather the tea towel corners and tie with a string to form a bag. Hang it over the sink or bowl, and the whey will drain freely.
Two things are happening while the curd drains. Acid is developing, so the flavor of the cheese is coming to life. The moisture ratio of liquid to solid is dropping, therefore the consistency and the stability of the finished product are changed. Chevre is meant to be soft, so the moisture level will remain high. This high moisture content makes chevre less stable than other aged or hard cheese, so it should be consumed within a few days after making. (This cheese will not improve with age and is meant to be eaten as a freshly made product).
Allow the curd to drain for 12 hours. Then remove it from the bag and place it in a bowl. Work in the salt. Salting has a number of purposes in the cheese-making process. It adds flavor, promotes the shedding of moisture, and retards bacterial growth.
Flavor with herbs such as fresh chives or a favorite, herbs de provence. This classic blend is an herb gardener's delight. You may adjust quantities of the various herbs according to your taste. After adding the salt and herbs, either enjoy immediately or refrigerate for storage (up to 7 days).

To pasteurize milk:
Equipment: Dairy thermometer, a double boiler, or two nesting pots
1. Pour the milk into the smaller of the two pots, and place the small pot inside the larger one, with three inches of water in the bottom of the large pot.
2. Slowly heat the milk to 145°F and hold the temperature there for 30 minutes. Stir the milk gently throughout the process to make sure it is evenly heated.
3. Remove the milk from the heat source and place the pan in a sink filled with ice, to bring the temperature down as quickly as possible. If you are ready to make this recipe, bring it down to 86°F and begin your cheese-making. If the milk is to be stored after pasteurized, bring it down to 40°F. Refrigerate until use.

Cheese-making ingredient source –
New England Cheese-making Supply, 54B Whately Road, South Deerfield, MA 01373, www.cheesemaking.com, Phone 413-397-2012, Fax 413-397-2014

Janet Hurst is the author of "Homemade Cheese," Voyageur Press, 2011 and "The Whole Goat Handbook," Voyageur Press, 2013. The recipe featured here is from "Homemade Cheese."

STONE HILL WINERY
HERMANN

Stone Hill Winery and Vintage Restaurant used to be a family home.

Thomas Held started slipping little plastic seals on wine bottles when he was two-and-a-half years old, and while he doesn't work on seals any longer at Stone Hill Winery, he's involved as its director of sales and advertising and works alongside his brother Jon, general manager, and parents Jim and Betty, owners of Stone Hill Winery. The scenic winery has long been a family effort.

"When someone comes into the winery, they are entering our home—literally, we lived upstairs for some 20 years," Thomas says. Today, a vineyard takes up the sunny slope approaching the brick house, now a winery tasting room and gift shop. The charming hilltop setting of Stone Hill is perfect for the many special events there: Maifest, the Cajun Concert on the Hill, the Big Band Dance, Oktoberfest, other Wine Trail events, and more. Daily, visitors can taste wines from the vineyards. "We've chosen to concentrate on Missouri's unique grape varieties," Held says, "like Norton and Chardonel, well adapted to our situation."

The approach seems to be working: in addition to other awards, Dave Johnson, senior winemaker, has generated seven Missouri Governor's Cup awards, more than 3,700 other wine awards, as well as the Missouri Grape and Wine Program's Pioneer Award, given to both Dave and Jim and Betty Held.

The winery, now listed on the National Register of Historic Places, has a storied past as well. Established in 1847, Stone Hill grew to be the second largest winery in the United States, winning gold medals in eight world's fairs. It shipped 1,250,000 gallons of wine per year at the turn of the century and before Prohibition stopped wine production. Then, the historic, vaulted cellars housed mushroom production for a time. In 1965, the Helds purchased the property and began rebuilding. A small section of the cellar was cleared out for wine, and gradually, they were instrumental in bringing the wine industry in Missouri back from its dormant state. Currently, Stone Hill Winery produces about 260,000 gallons of wine per year.

In another push, the family restored the winery's former carriage house and horse barn in 1979 into today's Vintage Restaurant, serving cuisine that includes many German specialties such as hot German potato salad, red cabbage, sauerbraten, sausages, and schnitzel. The tables are designed into what were Belgium horse stalls and feed troughs.

Cheeseburgundy Casserole
Serves 4-6

1 pound ground beef
⅓ cup onion, chopped
1 (10.5-ounce) can condensed tomato soup
¼ cup Stone Hill Norton or Hermannsberger
1 cup peas
Salt and pepper to taste
1 cup sifted flour
1-½ teaspoons double-acting baking powder
¼ teaspoon salt
2 tablespoons shortening
⅓ cup plus 1 tablespoon milk
8 cubes (¾-inch) American or cheddar cheese

Brown ground beef and onion in skillet; drain off fat. Add the tomato soup, wine, peas, salt, and pepper. Turn this mixture into 1-½ quart casserole.

Sift together the flour, baking powder, and salt in mixing bowl. Cut in shortening until particles are fine. Add milk and stir until dough clings together. Knead on lightly floured surface 12 times. Divide into 8 pieces. Mold the dough around cheese cubes and place on casserole. Bake at 425°F. for 25 to 30 minutes until a deep, golden brown.

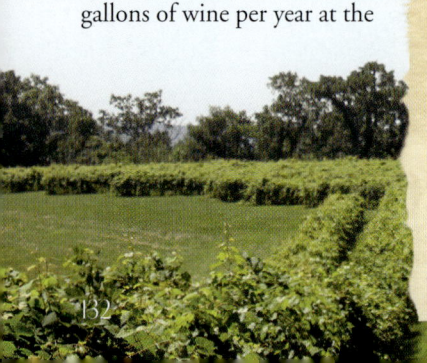

Dave Johnson (left) and Thomas Held

Stone Hill Winery
1110 Stone Hill Highway
Hermann, MO 65041

www.stonehillwinery.com
800-909-9463

Sundays:
10 a.m. - 6 or 6:30 p.m.*
Mondays - Thursdays:
8:30 a.m. - 6:30 or 7 p.m.*
Fridays - Saturdays:
8:30 a.m. - 7:30 or 8 p.m.*
*Depending on season

Open Thanksgiving Eve, Christmas Eve, and New Year's Eve until 5 p.m.

Closed Thanksgiving, Christmas, and New Year's Day

German Chocolate Pie
2 pies, serves 16, prepared by Marge Radtke of Stone Hill Winery & Restaurant

6 tablespoons margarine
⅔ cup semi-sweet chocolate chips
3 eggs
1 teaspoon vanilla
1-¼ cups sugar
1-½ tablespoons cornstarch

1 can evaporated milk
2 frozen 9-inch pie shells
½ cup coconut
¼ cup chopped pecans
Whipped cream, optional

Preheat oven to 350°F. Melt together margarine and chocolate chips in bowl over boiling water. In a bowl, mix together eggs and vanilla. Stir together sugar and cornstarch and add to egg mixture. Add chocolate mixture to egg and sugar mixture while mixing. Add evaporated milk and mix completely. Pour into pie shell that is frozen. Sprinkle coconut and pecans onto pie. Mix gently with fingers to cover coconut and pecans and distribute evenly in pie. Place pie onto baking sheet and bake approximately 35 to 45 minutes or until center of pie is set. Cool completely, cover tightly, and refrigerate. Can be frozen for later use.

Serving suggestion: Warm in microwave slightly above room temperature and top with fresh whipped cream.

SWISS MEAT AND SAUSAGE
HERMANN

The meat is cut fresh at Swiss Meat and Sausage.

The sign on Interstate 70 says they have the "Best of the Wurst," at Swiss Meat and Sausage in Hermann. And many people agree the sausages are worth the picturesque drive down Highway 19. What started in a country store and gas station in 1965 in the village of Swiss is now a family business with three generations at work.

Founder Bill Sloan remembers what it was like on the farm growing up near his grandparents in Sullivan when farmers did their own meat butchering, processing, and curing. At 15, Bill started work at an IGA grocery where families rented freezer lockers since there wasn't much home refrigeration, and he never looked back. He held on to one key memory, though: the good part of the business back then was that one butcher served one customer until they were satisfied. "If we didn't have the right cut of meat, we cut it." He did not go along with selling pre-cut, pre-wrapped meat. "Now butchers in stores are not even butchers, or even meat cutters; they are box openers."

At Swiss Meat and Sausage, the meat is fresh cut. Bill calls Glenn Brandt the wurstmeister and together with all the family tasters, they come up with unusually good brats. They offer 52 varieties of bratwurst and sausages like apple and cinnamon, mushroom and Swiss, chipotle, German-style summer sausage, braunschweiger, thuringer, Krakow, and andouille sausage. Then, there are hams, pork chops, jerky, turkey, and chicken, to choose from as well. In 2011, Swiss began offering Swiss Signature Brats for Mizzou Tiger Athletics, available at selected groceries statewide.

A stop at the Swiss Meat and Sausage store offers locally made jellies, jams, and a charming display of the Sloan family kitchen antiques. There are three full walls decorated with awards. Service is legendary and tours are welcome, especially with a call in advance.

A lot of family works at the business: Bill's daughters Sharon Fennewald, Deana Mundwiller, Janice Thomas, Vicki Slater, and granddaughters Liz and Becca Mundwiller. His son, Mike, opened his own shop, the Hermann Wurst Haus in Hermann, proving that Missouri flavors are in this family's blood.

Swiss Meat and Sausage Company
2056 S. Highway 19
Hermann, MO 65041

www.swissmeats.com
573-486-2086

Sundays:
11 a.m. - 4 p.m.
May through Dec. 24;
Closed Sundays after
Christmas through April
Mondays - Saturdays:
8 a.m. - 5 p.m.

Back row: Becca Mundwiller, Janice Thomas, Vicki Slater, Sharon Fennewald, Deana Mundwiller, Liz Mundwiller; front row: Bill and Pat Sloan

Maple Sausage & Blueberry Breakfast Treat
Serves 6-8

¼ cup sugar
1 tablespoon cornstarch
2 cups fresh or frozen blueberries
¾ cup maple syrup
1 tablespoon butter
2 cups pancake mix
1 egg, beaten
2 tablespoons canola oil
1 package Maple Syrup Breakfast Sausage

In a small saucepan, combine sugar and cornstarch with ½ cup water and the 2 cups of blueberries. Bring to a boil. Cook and stir until thickened. Stir in maple syrup and butter; set aside and keep warm. Combine 1 cup water with pancake mix, egg, and oil. Pour into a greased 13x9-inch baking dish. Brown the sausages in a skillet and arrange on top of the pancake batter. Pour the blueberry mixture over the top and bake, uncovered at 350°F for 30 to 40 minutes.

RICKY'S CHOCOLATE BOX

HERMANN

The candies are freshly made and hand-crafted at Ricky's Chocolate Box.

James Justus's interest in special effects makeup, sculpture, and ceramics has transmuted into chocolate creations: his Spotted Turtle has a caramel-infused belly, cashew legs, and a butter cookie shell. Plus, the treat looks as if it might wink at you. At Halloween, there could be ghouls working behind the counter at the Chocolate Box offering marshmallow eyeball cookies and cream Frankenstein heads.

James and his mother, Mary Hughey, have taken up the reins of their shop after father and husband Rick Hughey passed on. Rick was by all accounts a natural-born cook, and he created all his own recipes for the store they opened in 2004. The care James and Mary still take with Rick's concoctions is evident when you walk in the shop on Market Street in Hermann. The shop itself is quiet and not highly decorated. Mary and James focus all their attention on the trays of chocolate truffles, black and whites, clusters, and turtles. Once you step in the door, you won't have eyes for anything else.

Turtles come in all configurations here: Wild Blueberry Almond, Rare Albino, Butter Toffee Crunch, Pistachio, Cashew, Dark Apricot, Caramel Apple, and Pecan, among others. During October, Hermann's busiest month for visitors, trays of 80 to 120 truffles disappear regularly, going out the door in varying box sizes in the hands of pleased-looking customers.

In fact, everything at the Chocolate Box is freshly made on the spot and everything is hand-dipped and crafted. You'll find more than 60 items at any one time, with treats rotating seasonally: more cinnamon and spice options in the fall, berries and chocolate in the summer.

Ricky's Chocolate Box
310 Market Street
Hermann, MO 65041

www.rickyschocolatebox.com
573-291-6107

Sundays - Fridays:
10 a.m. - 4 p.m.
Saturdays:
10 a.m. - 5 p.m.
(6 p.m. during Octoberfest)

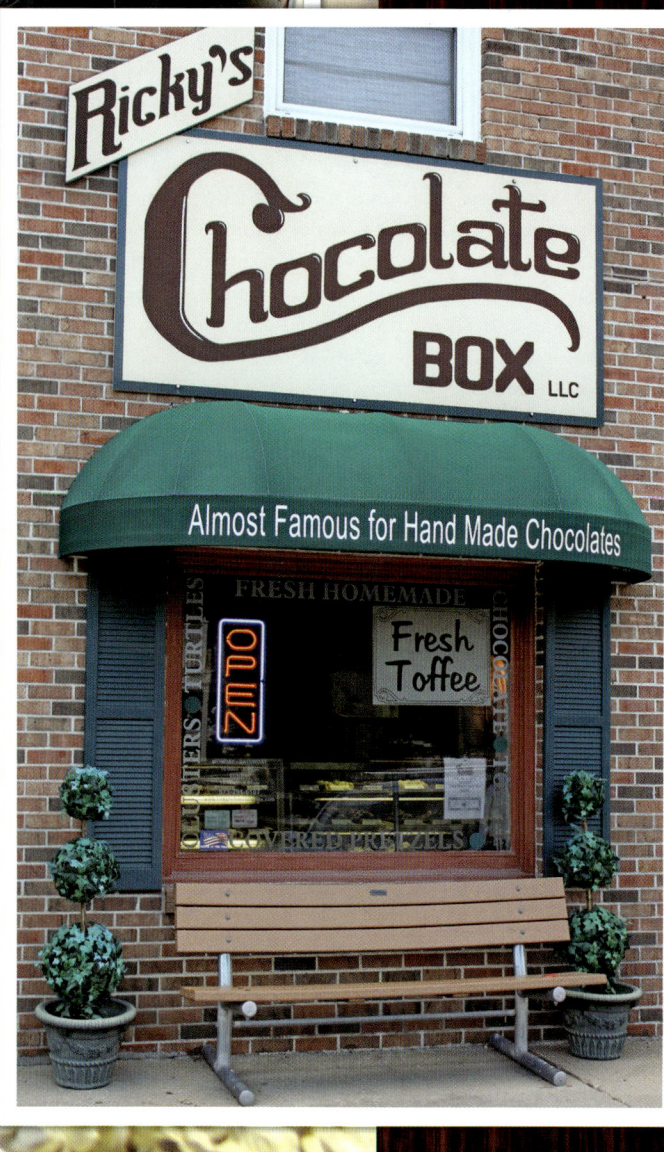

THE COTTAGE
HERMANN

The Cottage offers a farmers' market menu.

On 22 acres of woods in Hermann, Connie Keith and Sidney Miller create wonderful lunch and dinner experiences for their guests. The property's namesake 1940s cottage, adjacent garage, and barn were repurposed as a restaurant, gallery, and art studio in 2001. The patio is surrounded by dogwood trees and, when the sun is out, dotted with umbrellas over tables. Inside The Cottage, Sidney's husband's art brightens the light-filled rooms.

The Cottage's farmers' market menu includes foods such as pan-fried chicken, meatloaf with green tomato gravy, and Grandma Katie's Caramel Cake. Prime Rib is served every Friday and Saturday night. The cheese grits here have a kick of jalapeno, the cilantro pesto is fresh on the tongue, and the caramelized onion spread on crostini is addictive. Depending on the season, you may get a fresh fruit cobbler that is not too sweet, or orange liqueur cheesecake, or chocolate peanut butter pie. The owners also enjoy international foods and host dinners focusing on foods from different countries several times per year.

You feel you are in good hands once you step through the door even though Sidney did not grow up cooking. "My mother never let me in the kitchen except to do the dishwashing," she says. But now, she's making up for lost time. Connie was given a step stool when she was 10 years old to help out in the kitchen. Even today, the pie crust recipe she uses was her mother's.

The women came up with the idea for the restaurant when they took walks together as neighbors. "Sidney would make too much of a dish and bring it to share," Connie says. "We discovered both of us liked to cook."

The women are sensitive to what is seasonal and what local taste buds might crave. "We make fried green tomatoes at the *end* of tomato season—by then everyone's tired of their tomatoes," Connie says as she holds her arms out as if she's carrying a wide basket to indicate how many green tomatoes they get. "If a farmer brings in three pounds of shiitake mushrooms, we'll be doing vegetable sandwiches, steaks, and all kinds of things that pair well with mushrooms."

This flexibility extends to the seasoned staff, most of whom have been involved at The Cottage for eight years or more. The effect of all this is a happy experience for guests and a respite as you journey through the Hermann area.

Connie Keith (left) and Sidney Miller

The Cottage
1185 Highway H
Hermann, MO 65041

www.goodfoodfineart.com
573-486-4300

Call to check seasonal hours.

The Cottage Crostini with Fig Jam, Caramelized Onions, and Feta
Serves 6-8

2 cups white onions, sliced
1 tablespoon butter
¼ cup beef broth
¼ cup chicken broth
1 package mission figs
¼ cup sherry (optional)
French or Italian bread, thinly sliced, toasted
Feta cheese, crumbled

Melt the butter in a skillet and add the onions. Cook very slowly, stirring every 10 to 15 minutes, until all the liquid released by the onions has evaporated and they are light to medium brown in color. (The process will take several hours.) Add the beef and chicken broth and continue to cook slowly until the liquid has evaporated a second time.

To make the jam, cover the figs with water and cook slowly until soft. Do not drain. Place in a food processor, add sherry, if desired, and puree. Spread each bread slice with the caramelized onions, then with jam. Top with crumbled feta cheese.

Grandma Katie's Caramel Cake
Serves about 12

For syrup:
1 cup sugar
¾ cup boiling water

For cake:
3 eggs, separated
½ cup butter
2-½ cups sugar, divided
1 cup cold water
1 teaspoon vanilla
3 cups flour
¼ teaspoon salt
2-½ teaspoons baking powder
½ teaspoon baking soda
5 tablespoons burnt sugar syrup (recipe below)

For icing:
3 tablespoons burnt sugar syrup
3 cups sugar
1 cup cream
½ cup (1 stick) butter
pinch of salt
1 teaspoon vanilla
¾ teaspoon baking soda

Burnt Sugar Syrup:
Cook 1 cup sugar in a heavy skillet or pan over medium heat, stirring constantly until sugar is an amber color. Remove from heat and add ¾ cup boiling water. Stir until the mixture is a syrup. You might cover the skillet a bit when you start adding the water because it will spatter at first. Set mixture aside. This part can be done ahead and refrigerated for a day or so.

Caramel Cake:
Separate the eggs and beat the egg whites until stiff; set aside. Cream together butter and 1-½ cups sugar. Add the egg yolks to the butter and sugar and beat with an electric mixer until fluffy. Mix cold water and vanilla together; set aside. In a medium bowl, sift together the 3 cups flour, salt, baking powder, and baking soda; set aside. Alternately add dry and liquid ingredients to the creamed butter and sugar, beating well after each addition.

Add 5 tablespoons burnt sugar syrup and mix well. Fold in the 3 egg whites, beaten stiff. Pour into two greased and floured 9-inch cake pans or one 9x12-inch cake pan. Bake at 375°F for 30 to 35 minutes.

Burnt Sugar Icing:
Stir all ingredients except the baking soda together and place over medium heat. Stir constantly until mixture reaches a soft ball stage. Remove from heat and add baking soda. Beat until the right consistency to spread.

TIN MILL BREWERY
HERMANN

Tin Mill Brewery brews flagship and seasonal beer in the German style.

The 15-barrel system brewer Elijah Holt uses at Tin Mill Brewery in Hermann makes about 465 gallons per batch. The brewery opened in 2006 making varieties of handcrafted beer, and today, Tin Mill turns out 1,100 to 1,200 barrels a year.

Brewery owners Don Gosen, brewmaster, and Ellen Dierberg saw a need for a microbrewery in Hermann with its German-rich heritage. Tin Mill crafts its beers in traditional German style, importing malted barley from Germany and using no corn or rice in its recipes. The brewhouse is in a 100-year-old mill, complete with its old grain processing equipment upstairs, in the middle of Hermann's picturesque town of restored buildings and hilly streets.

There's a list of year-round flagship brews such as the German-style pilsner, Skyscraper, an unfiltered wheat Hefe-Weizen, the dark lager Midnight Whistle, amber Red Caboose, and the full-bodied Dopplebock. Rotating varieties might include Pomegranate Wheat or Imperial Pilsner. There are seasonal special beers, Maibock and Oktoberfest, too, to savor.

"Our beers are enjoyable and give people a chance to find their taste," Elijah says. The recipes get tweaked to best represent what the beer should be, he says. "I'm constantly changing things and looking for subtleties. I'm never finished."

Tin Mill Brewery
1st & Gutenberg
Hermann, MO 65041

www.tinmillbrewery.com
info@tinmillbrewery.com
573-486-2275

Open seven days a week with seasonally changing hours.

Elijah Holt (left) and Natasha Phillips

Red Caboose Pork Chops
Serves 6

4 tablespoons fresh ginger root
½ cup brown sugar
½ teaspoon salt
½ teaspoon pepper
1-2 bottles of Tin Mill Red Caboose beer
6 pork chops, thick cut

Gently chop fresh ginger root and put in a large container. Add brown sugar, salt, pepper, and beer. Mix until sugar is dissolved. Submerge pork chops in marinade; let stand in refrigerator overnight and through the day, 16 to 20 hours. Heat grill. When hot put the pork chops on. Cooking times will vary, approximately 20 minutes.

HERMANN WURST HAUS
HERMANN

Find 30 kinds of brats, German sausages, and a deli at Hermann Wurst Haus.

The Hermann Wurst Haus in Hermann offers German sausages, 30 or more varieties of bratwurst, and a sit-down deli area in what used to be an auto parts store. Mike and Lynette Sloan inaugurated the now open and airy space dedicated to meats produced on-site and many locally made jams, jellies, and pickles in September 2011, but sausage-making has been Mike's life since he was 10 years old and helping his father at the family business, Swiss Meat and Sausage, just south of Hermann. Mike's sausages have won more than 350 awards: Best of Show in smoked bratwurst, fresh bratwurst, fresh pork sausage, schatmargen, liverwurst, summer sausage, and jerky, and also National Grand Champion for German bologna and hickory-smoked bacon, among many others. Mike's philosophy: "It's a bacon world, and it should be."

The process is an art, Mike says. "You read books, and then throw away those books and start talking with the guys that came before you and you sit and have conversations about wurst. Then you start to put what they don't teach you in the book into your products. I started bumping up some seasonings to bring out the taste," he says.

"The awards are a benchmark to me. They tell me I'm doing what I'm supposed to be doing. I about fell out of my chair the first time I won National Champion. For every award I've won, there are probably 10 I haven't. You learn, you pay your dues."

Stop into the Hermann Wurst Haus and judge for yourself. You'll enjoy the open airy space and inviting lunch counter. Lynette and Mike both want to continue their heritage of Missouri flavors.

Hermann Wurst Haus
234 E. First Street
Hermann, MO 65041

www.hermannwursthaus.com
sloan1@centurylink.net
573-486-2266

Sundays:
10 a.m. - 4 p.m.
Mondays - Saturdays:
9 a.m. - 6 p.m.

Lynette and Mike Sloan

Krautburgers
Serves 6-8

1 pound ground beef
1 cup chopped onion
1-½ teaspoons garlic powder
Salt and pepper to taste
½ pound cabbage, finely shredded
1 pounds sauerkraut, drained
½ cup beef broth
½ pound shredded sharp cheddar cheese
1-½ pounds white bread dough
4 tablespoons melted butter

Preheat oven to 350°F. In a skillet, brown the meat. Add onions, garlic, salt, and pepper. Add cabbage, sauerkraut, and beef broth. Turn heat to medium-low and stir and simmer until cabbage is just cooked. Remove pan from the stove and let mixture cool. Then, stir in shredded cheese and mix well. Next roll out dough on a floured surface to ⅛-inch thickness. Cut rolled dough into 4-inch squares. Place 2 ounces of the meat, cabbage, and cheese mixture into the center of each dough square; wet edges and fold over to seal together. Bake for approximately 30 minutes or until brown. Remove from oven and brush tops with melted butter.

THIERBACH ORCHARDS & BERRY FARM
MARTHASVILLE

Pick your own cherries at Thierbach Orchards & Berry Farm.

What may be the only pick-your-own cherry orchard in the state sits on the hills just north of the Missouri River at Marthasville. Susie and Otto Thierbach's orchards have tart cherries, peaches, apples, blackberries, raspberries, blueberries, and more. They start pressing apples in September for their own cider and offer hayrides for groups and a petting zoo for small children.

In addition, Susie and Otto have a somewhat secret life. Both are trained musicians—Otto toured with the Tommy Dorsey Band playing trombone and still plays with a group of musicians in Hermann. Susie plays the violin with the Union Avenue Opera in St. Louis, at Webster University, and others places.

But in the early 1990s, Otto took breaks from touring by coming home to plant trees. Eventually, he stopped touring and began tending the orchard full time. By 1999, the Thierbachs were fully focused on the orchards.

The Thierbachs and their two children, Elise and Wesley, two dogs, and assorted goats and bunnies live amongst 12 acres of peaches, 12 acres of apples, three acres of blueberries and blackberries, plus raspberries and strawberries in other fields. There's one acre of cherry trees that form a dense canopy that Susie and daughter Elise call the "secret garden," with its shady hush of leaves.

The orchard seems settled and calm, though there are bursts of great effort, as well as steady, thorough maintenance through the season to make it all happen. Hills roll away toward the Missouri River bottoms, and lush foliage marks the distance in all directions. Ed and LaVerda Thierbach, Otto's parents, live nearby, and LaVerda's cherry pie, a completely different taste experience than a pie made with canned cherries from grocery stores, is one sublime pleasure: tart yet sweet with satisfying flavor.

"I like helping people learn how good fresh fruit is," Susie says, "Our orchard is for all ages. Grandkids to grandparents have a good time here."

Susie and Otto Thierbach and their children, Elise and Wesley

Ed and LaVerda Thierbach

Thierbach Market
18427 State Highway 47
Marthasville, MO 63357
636-433-2757

Thierbach Orchards
Pick Your Own
15885 Orchard Lane
Marthasville, MO 63357

www.thierbachorchards.com
info@thierbachorchards.com
636-433-2299

Check website for days and times when fruit is ready to pick.

Thierbach's Market
Open daily during apple and peach season,
9 a.m. - 6 p.m.

Cherry Pie
Serves 8

2 quarts freshly picked tart cherries, pits removed, enough to fill 4 cups
Pie crust for 2-crust pie
1-⅓ cups sugar
⅓ cup flour
½ teaspoon cinnamon
1-½ teaspoon butter

Preheat oven to 425°F. Pit cherries (Susie suggests using a paper clip to pop the pits out easily) and set aside. Line the bottom of a 9-inch pie plate with crust. In a separate bowl, combine the sugar, flour, and cinnamon. Gently stir the cherries into this mixture and pour into the pastry-lined pie pan. Dot with butter. Cover with the top crust and cut slits in the crust. Bake at 425°F for 35 to 45 minutes or until the crust is nicely browned and juice bubbles through the slits.

McKITTRICK MERCANTILE
McKITTRICK

The 1890s McKittrick Mercantile is once again a gathering place.

In the heyday of McKittrick, when the Missouri Kansas and Texas Railroad line was completed in the 1890s, the mercantile was a bustling place for the surrounding farmers and river people. It housed a general store, post office, and a large upstairs space for theater performances, church services, and community events. The building fell into disuse by 1945, but today, Joey Los and Rich Lauer are bringing back its earlier luster.

The tiny town, on the north bank of the Missouri River across from Hermann, has small Victorian houses lining streets that wind downhill from the state highway. Joey and Rich renovated the old building into today's Mercantile to create a space for food circles, contra dancing upstairs, and a bed and breakfast, among other things. The downstairs floor space is shared by starting businesses, and there is seating for about 40 people.

Joey is active in promoting the idea of linking supportive food producers and consumers, and she hosts a monthly food circle gathering at the Mercantile. She has been active in organizations like the Missouri Organic Association and others and feels the way to make sustainable agriculture work is by supporting good practices. Rich's extensive background in renovation projects was a big part of the finished look of the Mercantile, a standout in tiny McKittrick.

The result of the couple's efforts is a pleasing building with open airy spaces inside. The shelves carry local products with room to expand. On any given day, a cheese-making class might be held downstairs, or a felting class, while contra dancing is planned for the evening. The Mercantile is once again a gathering place.

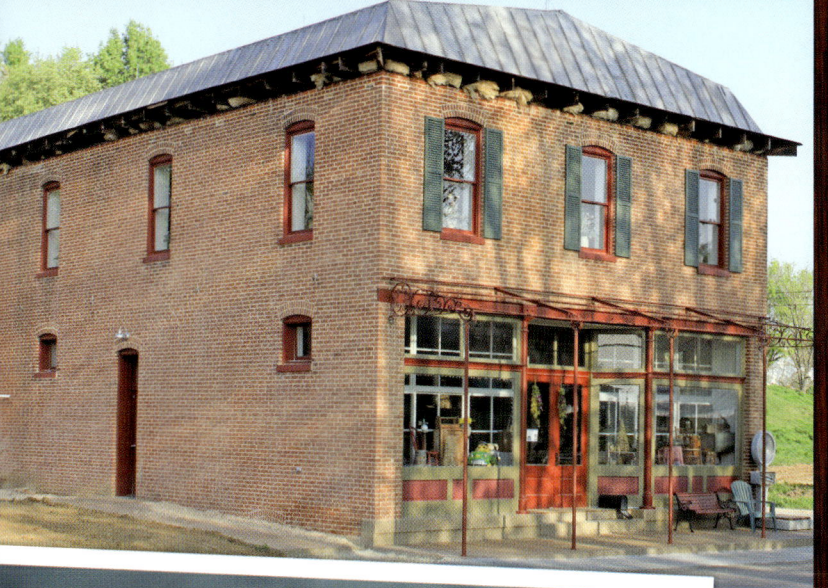

McKittrick Mercantile
500 Washington Street
McKittrick, MO 65041

www.themerck.com
mckittrickmercantile@
yahoo.com
573-486-2000

Hours change seasonally.
Check website for details.

McKittrick Merc Crustless Quiche
Serves 6-8

1 tablespoon oil or butter, divided
5-6 cups fresh greens (any kind, washed and coarsely chopped—try turnip, radish, chard, spinach, or other)
2 cups green onions, chopped (or one regular onion, finely chopped)
2 big carrots grated (about 1 cup) or substitute squash or pumpkin
1 tablespoon garlic, crushed
1 tablespoon dried basil, or small bundle fresh basil, or your favorite herbs finely minced
1-½ cups cottage cheese
¼ cup hard cheese or grated Parmesan cheese
¾ cup plain yogurt
5 large or 6 medium eggs
1 teaspoon salt, or to taste

Optional: add 1 cup finely chopped ham or bacon or leftover chicken. (This is a very versatile recipe!)

Preheat oven to 350°F. Lightly oil a heavy skillet with part of the oil and sauté greens until wilted. Let cool slightly. Mix with all other ingredients; mixture will be very thick. Lightly oil a deep-dish pie pan or shallow casserole dish, and pour mixture in. Bake until eggs are set in center. Let rest for 5 minutes before serving. This makes a delicious lunch with a side of fruit.

147

SASSAFRAS VALLEY FARM
MORRISON

Sassafras Valley Farm is home to the goose lady.

The goose lady of Gasconade County is down to earth, engaging, and ready to send you a goose or duck on demand. In 2007, Connie Cunningham decided to raise German Embden and French Toulouse geese on her family's farm near Morrison. She likes the sense of history a roast goose for the holidays gives people, and the fact that German and French settlers in the area would have raised these breeds for their own families. Along with her brother, Robert, who took on the marketing, website, and finance end of farm operations, she now raises and sells fresh frozen whole dressed geese as well as whole smoked geese via Internet sales for shipment across the country. In the past year, Connie began raising French Rouen ducks as well.

This focus is unusual deep in the heart of crop and cattle country. And Connie, who moved to the family farm after developing a landscape design business in Chicago, has learned by trial and error the ways of birds. She planted crab grass, dandelion, clover, and trefoil for the geese to graze, and she planted 40 pear trees after finding they like to clean up under the branches. She maintains low impact sustainable agricultural practices and finds the most challenging part of raising a flock is keeping them in clean water, sometimes changing tanks out twice a day in the summer heat.

The flock of geese roam peacefully as they graze on the rolling, lush hillsides of Sassafras Valley Farm. The geese seem pleased with their terrain but somehow vulnerable, honking occasionally, their feathers brightly white against the vivid green pasture. But Connie has yet to lose a goose or duck to predators, as the flock is protected by Connie's Great Pyrenees, Maximus and Angel.

The idyllic, tucked-away views of Sassafras Valley will soon be available to visitors interested in an overnight stay or perhaps a chef-on-the-farm dinner. Connie is renovating the original homestead into Sassafras Valley Bed and Breakfast with plans to open in Spring 2013. This will give more people a chance to see this slice of Missouri beauty. A stay here will include a chance to walk amongst birds of a feather.

Sassafras Valley Farm
Morrison, MO 65061

www.sassafrasvalleyfarm.com
866-684-2188

Farm tours and Bed and Breakfast by arrangement, call for reservation.

Connie's Roast Goose

1 goose

Lemons and oranges for stuffing

Spice Rub
1 orange peel, grated
1 tablespoon of salt
1 tablespoon cinnamon
2 tablespoons allspice
2 tablespoons ground poultry seasonings

Glaze
1 cup red wine
½ cup honey

Mix together the spice rub.

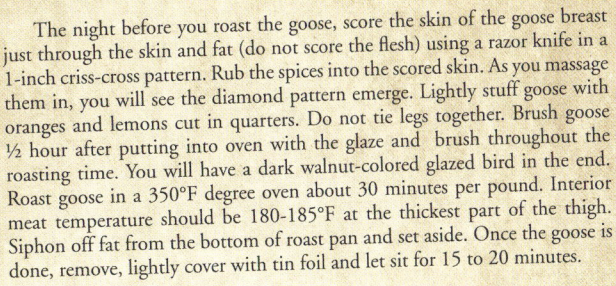

The night before you roast the goose, score the skin of the goose breast just through the skin and fat (do not score the flesh) using a razor knife in a 1-inch criss-cross pattern. Rub the spices into the scored skin. As you massage them in, you will see the diamond pattern emerge. Lightly stuff goose with oranges and lemons cut in quarters. Do not tie legs together. Brush goose ½ hour after putting into oven with the glaze and brush throughout the roasting time. You will have a dark walnut-colored glazed bird in the end. Roast goose in a 350°F degree oven about 30 minutes per pound. Interior meat temperature should be 180-185°F at the thickest part of the thigh. Siphon off fat from the bottom of roast pan and set aside. Once the goose is done, remove, lightly cover with tin foil and let sit for 15 to 20 minutes.

To carve a goose: Remove wings by breaking off at the joints, then remove legs in the same manner, leaving the prime part of the goose, the breast, accessible to slicing. Slice thinly as goose is rich.

Suggestion: Save the set-aside fat for frying potato pancakes the next day. These are wonderful served with sour cream and applesauce.

RIVER'S EDGE RESTAURANT
MORRISON

An old flour mill hosts River's Edge Restaurant.

Getting to River's Edge Restaurant near Morrison is an adventure. Though the address is listed as Morrison, locals shake their heads, no: it's Fredericksburg, population 14. The house specialties are Cajun-Creole: Shrimp Three Ways, Crab Two Ways, peel-and-eat shrimp, blackened chicken, steak, catfish, crab boil, and crawfish. Side choices include red beans and rice, seafood gumbo, and okra.

River's Edge sits right on the Gasconade, nine miles from the mouth of the Missouri River, and the old ferry dock is at its feet. The restaurant is a three-story, 19th-century flour mill with a colorful past. For a time, it housed an ice house, a fishing and hunting lodge, and during Prohibition, a bootleg operation. Once there, you will be able to visualize this past, a little dark, likely lively.

For as large a building as it is, the rooms are cozy with exposed rock walls and large square-timbered supports and beams. The atmosphere is very casual, two rooms inside, outdoor deck outside. Couples walk in, greet the bartender by name, and settle in for their favorites. A platter of catfish emerges from the kitchen, and the aroma is tantalizing. Linda and Steve Simmons, proprietors, also run Simmons on the Waterfront in Hermann. At River's Edge, they serve up nicely spiced gumbo, charbroiled shrimp, and bread in a clay pot with honey butter. The house sweet-and-sour salad dressing is light and only slightly sweet, avoiding the cloying taste of some dressings like this. Other sauces the Simmons create include Orange Cajun Sauce, Sizzlin' Pepper Sauce, and Raspberry Jazz. It is worth the drive to this tucked-away spot and local flavor, up from the south.

River's Edge Restaurant
1720 Old Ferry Road
Morrison, MO 65061

573-294-7207

Sundays:
Noon - 8 p.m.
Fridays:
4 p.m. - 10 p.m.
Saturdays:
4 p.m. - 10 p.m.

PINCKNEY BEND DISTILLERY
NEW HAVEN

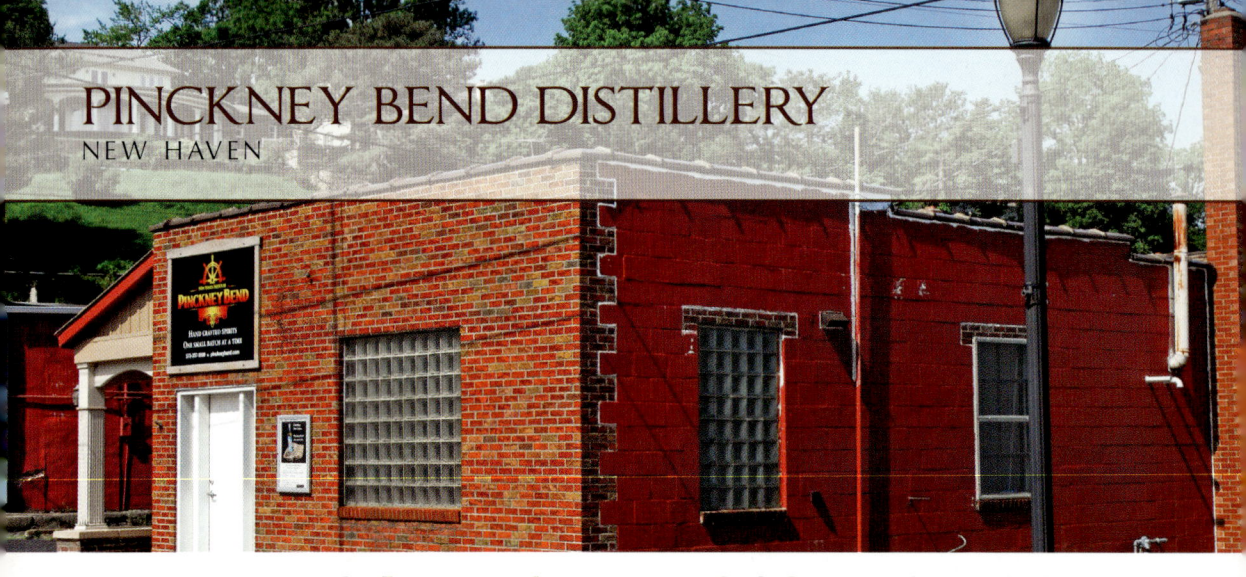

Namesake distillery near where Lewis and Clark stopped for a drink.

by contributor Kaitlin Steinberg

The story goes that in 1806, Lewis and Clark plotted a route past the hazard that would become known as Pinckney Bend, and bought two gallons of whiskey from trappers a few miles down the river. They chafed at the $8 cost of the spirits, but not the quality.

Enjoying the historical tie, three friends dreamed up Pinckney Bend Distillery: CEO Jerry Meyer, distiller Tom Anderson, and marketing guru Ralph Haynes, who says they used the location's history as a jumping off point. The distillery opened to the public in summer 2012.

Though the old town of Pinckney was washed away by flood in 1824 and then succumbed to the elements when the river changed direction some years later, its spirit remains. Today, New Haven sits across the Missouri River from where the town of Pinckney once welcomed guests with whiskey and other distilled spirits.

"We named the distillery Pinckney Bend to evoke a sense of provenance, of being from a place," Ralph says.

Pinckney Bend Distillery is located just a short walk from the levee, where you can look out on the Missouri River and imagine the bustling docks of Pinckney on the opposite shore, perhaps loading whiskey to ship downstream. Further inland from the distillery is historic downtown New Haven with quaint shops facing the railroad tracks. In this part of New Haven, life moves a little slower, and all the neighbors and business owners greet each other by name. There are a number of bed and breakfasts in old homes along the river, perfect for relaxing after tasting local wine and spirits.

With a moustache to rival Colonel Sanders and the disposition to match it, Ralph is the guy who travels to nearby vendors to introduce new customers to his products (and maybe even to do a little tasting himself).

His passion for spirits is evident in his excitement to introduce them to others, especially the distillery's gold medal-winning gin, which beat out larger, more established companies to take home top honors at the 2012 San Francisco International Spirits Competition. In addition to their handcrafted American gin, Pinckney Bend also produces vodka, and they plan to start marketing aged whiskey and a few liqueurs once they've established themselves. It is their goal to put Pinckney Bend Distillery on the map and introduce the historic area to a new generation of liquor aficionados.

Pinckney Bend Distillery
Miller Street, Downtown
New Haven, MO 63068

www.pinckneybend.com
573-237-5559

Check website for hours of operation.

Gin Rickey

A classic old 19th-century cocktail with a good story: Gin Rickey was named after a Col. Joe Rickey of Missouri, who was a lobbyist in Washington, D.C., in the 1880s.

1 tablespoon sugar
Juice of half a lime
1 lime wedge for garnish
1-½ ounce Pinckney Bend American Gin
Carbonated water

Dissolve sugar in gin. Pour gin and lime juice into a highball glass over ice. Fill with carbonated water and stir. Add the lime wedge and enjoy.

RÖBLLER WINERY
NEW HAVEN

Enjoy the view and the wine at Röbller Winery.

If you stand on Röbller Winery's hillside, take in the 360-degree-view: rolling Missouri for miles. It's worth a twirl, or two. It may be enough to come here just to see the panoramic view, but then you get the treat of wine.

In 1987, Robert and Lois Mueller took a drive, leaving from their home in Glendale, found a spot worth visiting with good soils, and planned their vineyard on its hills. After making home wines since 1965, to the increasing pleasure of friends, and visiting California's wine country to learn more about wines, Robert could visualize a vineyard with good air circulation around vines and sunlit slopes. A draw, too, was that the property still boasted a house built in 1821 and the history of the land was marked by Civil War skirmishes.

Soon the Muellers made it home. All four children, Sue, Jerry, Mary and Beth, along for the ride on that fateful day in 1987, still work on the property: Jerry works alongside Robert in the Vineyard and cellar, Beth finds unique items for the gift shop, Sue is the site nurse for special events, and Mary does the advertising sales and helps coordinate music. All help with special events.

On 16 acres of producing vineyard, the Muellers cultivate Vidal, Vignoles, Seyval, Traminette, Steuben, Villard Noir, St. Vincent, Chambourcin, and Norton grape varieties. The three school teachers out for a holiday while I was there stopped and smiled mid-tasting. Their verdict? It's all good.

Röbller Winery
275 Robller Vineyard Road
New Haven, MO 63068

www.robllerwines.com
573-237-3986

Sundays:
Noon - 5 p.m.
Mondays - Saturdays:
10 a.m. - 5 p.m.

Closed some holidays.

Jerry Mueller (left) and Robert Mueller

Röbller Holiday Chutney
Makes about 5-6 cups

1-½ cup fruity red wine
1-½ cup sugar, divided
1 cup dried cranberries, chopped
2 cups cherry Craisins, divided
1-½ cup dried cherries
½ cup orange juice
½ cup white wine vinegar

3 tablespoons lemon juice
¼ teaspoon ground ginger
½ teaspoon ground cloves
¼ teaspoon crushed red pepper
1 cup tart apple, finely chopped
1-½ cup celery, finely chopped

Combine red wine and ½ cup sugar in a sauce pan. Simmer over low heat for 10 minutes. Add chopped cranberries and 1 cup cherry Craisins and simmer for an additional 20-30 minutes.

In a microwave safe mixing bowl, combine dried cherries, remaining Craisins, 1 cup of sugar, orange juice, vinegar, lemon juice, ginger, cloves, and red pepper. Stir until sugar is dissolved. Microwave on high for 4 minutes; stir and microwave on high for another 4 minutes.

Pour both mixtures into a stock pot and simmer on medium heat for 10 minutes. Stir in apples; simmer for another 10 minutes. Stir in celery and remove from heat. Let cool; then refrigerate. Serve chilled over roasted turkey, duck, or pork, or serve with mild white cheese on crackers.

SECOND SHIFT BREWING
NEW HAVEN

What started with a home-brewing kit turned into Second Shift Brewing.

Steve Crider has a lot on his plate: crafting beers, marketing product, adjusting brews. "It's all in the taste," he says. Steve, a welder, fabricator, and machinist, made his first batch of artisan beer for commercial sale in November 2010, but it started with a home-brewing kit given to him as a Christmas gift in 1999. "I was in deep within a matter of months."

Today, Steve markets traditional Belgian-style wheat beers, big hoppy beers (what he calls "big hop-forward American brews"), seasonal beers ("odd, goofy beers"), and more. His brews have names such as Cat Spit Stout, Art of Neurosis, and Unicorn Killer. When talking about his wheat beer, he mentions orange peel and coriander, traditional to him, and his addition of hibiscus flowers to "make it tart and a little pink."

He brews a beer many times; for Art of Neurosis, he "probably brewed it as many as 40 times," making adjustments before approving the taste and recipe, hence the name. The Second Shift website lists the beers as well as the type of hops—Centennial, Simcoe, Columbus, Cascade, Amarillo—used in each beer. A few minutes with Steve will give you an insight on what he loves about brewing.

"The art and science of it—it's just as much one as the other. Plus, I get to make more flavorful craft beers because I'm brewing on a smaller scale" than large commercial breweries.

In 2010, Second Shift Brewing was the smallest brewer in Missouri, making 31 gallons. In 2011, it was up to 250 gallons. In 2012, he predicted 864 gallons, and he can't keep up with demand. The beer house and Steve's new tasting room, opened in 2012, is tucked behind the Cedar Creek Conference Center in New Haven.

Second Shift Brewing
1401 Olive Road
New Haven, MO 63068

www.2ndshiftbrewing.com
steve@2ndshiftbrewing.com
573-237-3421

Tasting Room Hours:
Saturdays - Sundays:
Noon - 7 p.m.

LES LAVANDES
STARKENBURG

Take in a European high tea at Les Lavandes.

On a winding, wooded road just past the Our Lady of Sorrows Shrine and Church at Starkenburg, Les Lavandes Bed and Breakfast and Tea House offers European high tea. Myrta Weber creates tasty treats that will perk up your taste buds while you sip unusual drinks like linden tea.

"I am a baker's daughter," Myrta says. While growing up in Switzerland, she watched her father bake, and now she recreates tastes of her original Swiss home for visitors in Missouri. "It is a nice welcome to people," she says, "an ice breaker between guests and ourselves."

After retiring from nearly 30 years as a stewardess for Swissair, TWA, and then American Airlines, she felt she needed to stay active. Together with her husband, Richard, who retired from a career dealing in hardwood flooring, they decided to open Les Lavandes in 2003. They both love providing hospitality to guests and enjoy interacting with people from various backgrounds.

Lavender plants grow in Myrta's garden, withstanding even Missouri's strong weather. She uses the fragrant blossoms in various pastries and in her delicate ice cream.

The day I visited, she served Linzer tart, composed of elderberries, blackberries, and black raspberries she picked herself, some right out of her garden. There were chocolate-covered strawberries, raspberry chocolate truffles, and more. All were served on a lace-covered table in a room with lots of windows looking out over rolling views.

The house is 140 years old and used to be the Starkenburg post office. The living room, though now remodeled, was a general store in its past life. Today, when guests arrive, they find an inviting bed and breakfast. Richard is the chef in the mornings and sometimes at dinners, depending on what is requested. His favorite of Myrta's baked goods? Lavender cookies.

Les Lavandes Bed & Breakfast and Tea House
215 Highway P
Starkenburg
Rhineland, MO 65069

www.leslavandesbandb.com
leslavandesbb@gmail.com
573-236-4774

Dinner or High Tea
by appointment

Lavender Ice Cream

2 cups whipping cream
2 cups half and half
1 cup sugar
1 teaspoon vanilla
2 teaspoons fresh lavender flowers

Combine all ingredients and process in an ice cream maker until set.

ROLLING MEADOWS VINEYARD
WARRENTON

A teacher finds it therapeutic to share his winemaking craft.

by contributor Gretchen Jameson

It could be the teacher in him or that he grew up on a nearly century-old Michigan family vineyard that gives Missouri winemaker and vintner Ed Staude his unique ability to keep the art and science of wine approachable.

Whatever the reason, Rolling Meadows Vineyard & Winery, operated by Ed and Claudia Staude, is a delightfully unexpected stop before reaching Missouri's more established wine trails.

Rolling Meadows, aptly located on Eden Trail just west of Warrenton, is a working winery where wine lovers and casual enthusiasts alike can experience the craft of winemaking.

In every season, you can usually find Ed tending the tasting room or working the vines. Guests enjoy a rare opportunity to watch a true winemaker at work: pruning, trimming, bottling, harvesting, and crushing.

But Ed is never too busy to visit. "Although I'm not a talker by nature," he admits. "My wife is the more conversational of the two of us." Still, drop by Rolling Meadows, and you'll find Ed behind the table pouring and sharing the craft of his wines or leading enthusiastic patrons out into the vines or the barrel room for a quick tour.

"People are always curious about the process," he says. "We meet lots of folks who say they'd like to try this when they retire."

But it not as easy as it looks, Ed says. "Vineyard tending is gentleman farming, and I suppose that sounds easy, but when our guests learn that each RMV vine is hand-tended and touched at minimum four times per year, you see people do the math and recognize the amount of work it takes to make that glass of wine so memorable."

Rolling Meadows produces four distinct varietals: two whites, including Niagara, a sweet variety, and Seyval Blanc, a French hybrid; and two reds, including a sweet Concord and a venerable Missouri Norton.

One hundred percent of the grapes going into the wine made at Rolling Meadows are grown in the winery vineyards, made into wine, and bottled on site.

"We're a small operation, and so we operate by hand for very practical reasons, but it's definitely a distinction for our wines, and we're proud of it."

Ed was tending vineyards as part of a family operation from the time he was old enough to be in the vineyard. But life has taken him far from his Michigan roots. A teacher in Missouri since 1982, Ed chairs the humanities department at Lutheran High School of St. Charles County. The Staudes bought the property in 1998, following the passing of Ed's mother, and he established Rolling Meadows in 2000.

"I suppose building this place was my version of therapy," Ed explains.

Rolling Meadows Vineyard and Winery
212 Eden Trail
Warrenton, MO 63383

www.rmvwinery.com
rmvwinery@gmail.com
636-288-1016

Saturdays:
11 a.m. - 5 p.m.
and by appointment

FISTER FARM
WASHINGTON

Fister Farm features chickens, goats, and olive-oil soap.

The two story white farmhouse built in 1905, the sprawling red barn, the rolling hillside, and clucking chickens at Fister Farm near Washington all add up to lush and soothing pastoral views. There are sleeping dogs on the worn plank floors, and country music is often playing. On the farm, Fran and Neal Fister raise about 300 chickens for their eggs, six Nubian goats for their milk, and seven alpacas for their personalities and yarn. The pastoral views are soothing to family and visitors, and the animals seem pleased.

The Fisters, both raised in St. Louis, are refurbishing the farmhouse, though the bones of the place—high ceilings, wide plank flooring, and paned windows—need little enhancement. "I think the people who built this house were happy," Fran says. "I haven't had any ghosts or anything tell me otherwise." Fran, a nurse anesthetist, and Neal, an architect, commute: she to Fenton, and he to downtown St. Louis. The drive? Not bad, Neal says, "especially when what you come home to is this."

Farm life, Fran says, appeals to them because they wanted to provide their children with wholesome foods. Even before finding Fister Farm, they put in a garden, started an orchard, and began raising chickens. When the development they lived in became too closed-in, they moved. "I'm glad I've got kids that enjoy wide open spaces," Fran says.

The Fisters built shelters for the chickens, rolling houses for roosting and two hoop houses for nesting and laying. Fran collects about 25 dozen eggs each day that go to markets in St. Louis and Washington. She likes varied breeds: Barred Plymouth Rock, Red Leghorns, Golden Comets, and talks with them as she takes eggs from nesting boxes. We stop and take a look at the field: the green pasture is stippled with pecking hens, sunlight catching their color as they move from shade to open field. "That's why I like all the different breeds. I think it looks nice."

Fran's other project, "The Old Homestead" goat milk and olive oil soaps, are handmade and fragrant with grapefruit or lavender and come in five-ounce bars.

Fister Farm
766 Turning Leaf Drive
Washington, MO 63090

fister@toast.net
314-920-0004

By appointment, groups preferred

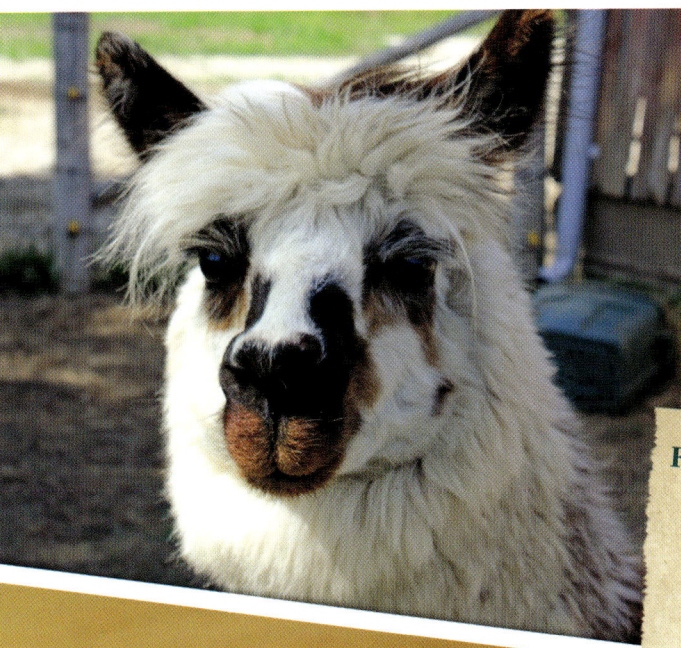

Fran's Grand Omelette
Serves 8-10

1 pound lean sausage
12 eggs
2 teaspoon seasoned salt
2 teaspoons paprika
1 cup evaporated milk
4 cans whole green chiles
1 ½ pound shredded Monterey jack cheese

Grease and flour a 9x13-inch baking dish. Fry sausage on the stove top until cooked through, drain excess fat and set aside. Beat eggs in a medium-sized bowl; add spices and milk. Layer cheese and green chiles in the prepared baking dish. Pour eggs over cheese and chiles. Layer fried sausage on top. Bake at 325°F for about 30 minutes or until firm and bubbly.

SCHULTE BAKERY
WASHINGTON

Schulte Bakery has made donuts, bread, and cookies since 1959.

The smell draws you closer to the counter at Schulte Bakery. Ah yes, donuts. Judy Thomas has been working in the bakery since day one in 1959: first with her father and mother, then her late brother, Leo, and now with her brother Paul. Judy's sister Alice and her husband, Al, also come and help on weekends. Alice, too, used to work in the bakery when she was a child.

It's a family that rolls out the dough, cuts the donuts, and makes the fillings and icings on site. Nothing comes out of a freezer. The custard filling for the doughnuts? Yep. The chocolate icing? Oh yeah. You can taste the difference, and you'll want to drop by to do so.

Children go straight for the decorated cookies, some in shapes of airplanes or frogs. If the shop runs out, Judy says, you can see their faces fall. The bakery also makes breads—white, French, wheat, rye, and multigrain—coffee cakes, pies, and layer cakes. Customers remember a time when Schulte's bread loaves were 15 cents apiece and they reminisce with Judy about those days. Judy watches the second generation of Schulte customers choose the same kind of pastries they grew up watching their parents choose. Judy remembers what their mom and dad liked best. It's that kind of place.

Some Sundays there are lines out the door for a solid hour and things get picked over. So be sure to get there before 10 a.m.

Schulte Bakery
1100 W. 5th St
Washington, MO 63090

636-239-2300

Tuesdays - Fridays:
6 a.m. - 2 p.m.
Saturdays:
6 a.m. - 1 p.m.
Sundays:
7 a.m. - Noon

TODD GEISERT FARMS
WASHINGTON

Todd Geisert Farms sells pastured pork and produce at their self-service farm stand.

"If the sun's up, we're open," Todd Geisert says of his self-service roadside produce and pork stand open 365 days a year. Drivers pull in front of the Geisert Farms barn on Old Highway 100 east of Washington, on the way to town, or on the way back, and choose naturally raised pork and seasonal produce harvested just steps away. You can pick your own herbs, too, just to the side of the barn. There's a weigh scale, hand-lettered price signs, and a money box for payments on the honor system. Most often, Todd himself is out working the farm, though he may stop and talk with a customer or two as he passes the barn.

The system works. In a 20-minute span of time, eight vehicles pull up and customers make their selections, fold bills into the money box, and leave carrying bags of tomatoes, zucchini, bacon, and more. Many times, old customers show new ones how to weigh their choices and where to pay.

The Geiserts have been producing hogs on this farm since 1916, and they added seasonal produce more recently. The original farmhouse sits across the highway from the pork and produce stand and overlooks the Missouri River. It's a beautiful view from there, and the farm is rich in family history. The Schultz family built the home in 1887, and Ben Geisert married a daughter of the house in 1916. Ben went to the University of Missouri; a lot of people at the time chuckled over his going to college to learn to farm. His terrace system became successful, though, and people started to take notice.

Today, Todd runs a 150-sow operation from farrow to finish, or about 1,000 hogs on a rotational pasture system that uses sunshine and space that creates little or no odor or problems with waste. Todd's grandfather started the system. "It's simple and it works," Todd says. Because of this, not much has changed in the way hogs have been raised here for nearly 100 years. Pigs are farrowed in A-frame houses that are moved seasonally, and crops are harvested from those fields in the next season.

Most confinement pig farms have 50,000-plus sows, Todd says, so Geisert Farms is considered small.

The Geiserts offer naturally raised pork: pork chops, pork sausage patties, pork burgers, brats, ribs, center-cut ham, and more. In 2008, the first year Todd took over farming from his father, D. John Geisert, he added tomatoes. That year Todd planted 120 tomato plants, and when he put the freshly picked tomatoes out on the stand each day at 7 a.m., they were gone by 10 a.m. The next year, he planted 800 plants and got the same results. Then, he tried 3,000 plants, then 4,500 plants, and got the same results. "On a slow day, we sell about 300 pounds of tomatoes," he says. Plus, there are peppers, squash, sweet corn, pumpkins, and more that sell in their season.

The farm method allows the Geiserts to do their own private-label pork products, sell their naturally raised premium meats to Niman Ranch, and keep their self-service stand open year-round. "I like trying to hang on to the tradition," Todd says. "I like dealing with sows and pigs," he says and then nods and laughs as he passes a field of vegetables, "I like planting it and selling it. I don't like weeding it and picking it."

Tomato Garlic & Basil Pork Chops
Geisert Family Recipe; serves 4-8

- 4-8 naturally raised pork chops, preferably 1-inch thick
- ½ cup canola oil, (water can be used as an option but does not create as much flavor)
- 1 package McCormick's Grill Mates, Tomato, Garlic & Basil Marinade

Defrost the pork chops, wash them, and pat dry. Mix the oil with the entire packet of seasoning. Brush the pork chops liberally with the oil seasonings. Bake pork chops at 350°F, reapplying the seasonings, until just pink inside, medium rare. Finish off under the broiler to give it a nice crisp color. Pork chops should still be slightly pink inside when removing them from the oven. Let sit for a few minutes, and they will finish cooking.

For smaller amounts, mix less seasonings and oil.

Todd Geisert Farms
4851 Old Hwy 100
Washington, MO 63090
(on Old Hwy 100, One
mile East of Fifth Street)

www.toadspigs.com
toadspigs@yahoo.com
314-791-6942

Farm Stand
Open daily sunrise to sunset

Todd Geisert (left) and D. John Geisert

Spinach Egg Casserole
Makes 6 servings

Cooking spray
1 small onion
½ cup red pepper, chopped
2 cups mushrooms, chopped
4 cups fresh spinach, torn
1 pound pork sausage
1 (6-ounce) package stuffing mix
2 tablespoons fresh parsley, chopped
6 eggs
¾ cup shredded mozzarella cheese

Preheat oven to 375°F. Grease a 9x13-inch baking pan and set aside. Spray a large skillet with cooking spray. Add onion, red pepper, and mushrooms; cook and stir on medium high for 5 minutes or until soft. Stir in spinach; set aside. Brown sausage and drain; set aside.

Prepare stuffing mix as directed on package; stir in onion mixture and parsley. In a medium bowl, beat eggs; mix with stuffing, sausage, and onion mix. Pour into the prepared baking pan and sprinkle with cheese. Bake 35 minutes or until firm. Cool 15 minutes before cutting into strips or squares. Serve warm.

Variation: Substitute 3 cups chopped asparagus for spinach.

WILLIAMS BROTHERS MEATS
WASHINGTON

Five generations lead to tasty creations at Williams Brothers in Washington.

Steve Williams is the fifth generation in his family's business with brothers Dan, Christopher, and Brian also at work in Williams Brothers Meats in Washington. It's a family that cares about the business, and it shows. The retail shop is inviting, filled with goods made on site, many times from local producers of pork, beef, and chicken. There are award-winning summer sausages hanging from the ceiling, and a savory aroma fills the air from the lunch specials behind the counter. Things are made the old-fashioned way here. And the people are friendly while doing it.

Meats have been a family focus for years. The brothers' maternal great-grandfather, Clancy, was a meat cutter from Ireland and just after World War II started a packing company in St. Louis. Later, their uncle ran two meat markets in the city. When the uncle had twelve children, Steve thought it would be tough to add one more in that business, so he came to Washington in 1982 and purchased Norv's Meat Shop. Steve kept some of the old recipes and began creating his own. Now, there is an average of 40 or 50 types of sausage, ham, bacon, and bratwurst offered. New flavors, such as an all-chicken, sun-dried tomato, and asiago cheese bratwurst they call the Mediterranean, or the Kentucky Bourbon Bratwurst, or Apple Cinnamon Bratwurst, are tried and kept if popular with customers.

These meat makers are a congenial lot. Everyone seems to smile here when they talk. Eyes crinkle with welcome when a customer comes in the door. Steve uncurls a hand-written list and confirms an order with his nephew while we talk. Then he continues, "It's hard to make meats this way," he says of the old-fashioned process of fermenting summer sausage. "We still put Norv's name on it. Not a lot of people know how to do this well."

The key seems to be time-tested experience. As Steve hands me samples of an Italian-fermented sausage, about a dime in diameter and dried hard, he tells me about the ethnic origins of various sausage traditions. Flavor bursts in my mouth as he says it's not just the Germans that know sausage. The Irish-German mix in the Williams family proves that.

Williams Brothers Meats
607 W. 5th Street
Washington, MO 63090

www.williamsbrothersmeats.com
wbmeats@gmail.com
636-239-2183

Mondays - Fridays:
8 a.m. - 7p.m.
Saturdays:
8 a.m. - 4 p.m.

Steve Williams

Acknowledgments

First, this book could not have happened without the generous gift of time by the people featured in *Savor Missouri*. They often rearranged their busy schedules so we could talk and delve into the details of their work. Many let me follow them around for several hours and for that, a heartfelt thank you. It could not have happened without you, and I hope the book does justice to all you do.

My thanks go to my publishers, Danita Allen Wood at *Missouri Life* and Doug Sikes at Acclaim Press, for giving me the opportunity to do this book. Bravo, too, to Sarah Herrera for her wonderful food photography that brings the recipes to life so well.

As always, I am deeply thankful for all the support of my husband, Terry, daughter, Anna, and son, Nathan. I was able to share a portion of an interview trip with Nate, a recipe or three with Anna, and great samples of Missouri sausages with Terry, and it made my summer.

To all those professional friends, mentors, and kind inquirers whom I encountered along the way: you are appreciated, always.

Nina Furstenau
Fayette, April 2013

Adam Puchta Winery in Hermann, Missouri

Index

A
Aartful Rose 68
Adam Puchta Winery 100, 124, 125, 171
Alfred Nahn Winery 110
Allen, James 60, 61
Allen, Pat 60, 61
Altenburg, MO 52, 53
Anderson, Tom 152
Appellation Cafe 112
Ashley's Rose Restaurant 100, 102, 103
Augusta Brewing Company 60, 100, 104, 105
Augusta, Missouri 102, 103, 104, 105, 106, 107, 108, 109, 111, 110, 112, 113, 114, 115
Augusta Winery 100, 106, 107, 108
Augusta Wine Trail 106, 114

B
Babbitt, Dennis 40, 41
Babbitt Honey 24, 40, 41, 42
Baetje Farms 50, 56, 57
Baetje, Steve 56
Baetje, Veronica 56
Bankhead Chocolates 24, 26, 27
Bankhead, Thomas Jefferson 26
Bat Creek Brewery 24, 28, 29
Beatty, Chuck 28
Beggs, Heather 78
Beggs, LaDonia 78, 79
Begg's Pioneer Market and Pick Your Own 78, 79
Beggs, Sam 78
Beggs, Stanley 78, 79
Belmonte, Michael 122
Benton, Missouri 54, 55
Berger, Missouri 116, 117, 119, 120, 121
Bias, Jim 116
Bias, Norma 116
Bias Winery 100, 116, 119
Blechle, Connie 80
Bloomsdale, Missouri 56, 57
Bock, Larry 126, 127
Bock, Ruth 126
Bolka, Nina 106, 112, 114
Bowling Green, Missouri 26, 27, 28, 29, 30, 31
Braggadocio, Missouri 62
Brandt, Glenn 134
Brazeau, Missouri 58, 59
Breezy Ridge Alpaca Farm 50, 80, 81
Bruckerhoff, Clyde 98, 99
Bruckerhoff, Jim "Trapper" 98, 99
Buckridge Farm Peaches 100, 126, 127
Burger, Morris 30
Byers, Clayton 108

C
Cape Girardeau, Missouri 8, 52, 54, 60, 61, 62, 63, 64, 65, 66, 67, 68, 69
Cape Girardeau Farmers' Market 67
Cape Riverfront Market 67
Carrow, Barbara 14
Cave Vineyard 50, 84, 85
Cedar Crest Manor 32
Celebrations 50, 60, 61
Centennial Farms 100, 110, 111
Centralia, Missouri 28
Champion, David 97
Champion, Leah 97
Champion, Michelle 96, 97
Charleville Vineyard, Winery and Microbrewery 50, 60, 86, 87
Chaumette Vineyards and Winery 50, 88, 91
Christmas Tree and Yule Log Cabin 70
Clarksville, Missouri 32, 33
Clayton Farmers' Market 57
Colony Flea Market 36
Colony, Missouri 36
Columbia, Missouri 128
Commean, Angela 33
Commerce, Missouri 70, 71
Cook, Sarah Beggs 78
Country Pastry Shop 24, 36, 37
County Line Farm 50, 98, 99
Crider, Steve 156
Crowley's Ridge 70
Crown Valley Brewery 92, 95
Crown Valley Farmers' Market 92
Crown Valley Winery and Brewery 50, 92, 95
Crystal City Farmers' Market 97
Cuba, Missouri 12, 13, 16, 17
Cunningham, Connie 148
Cunningham, Robert 148

D
Daffron, Heather 28
Daffron, Ryan 28
Danner, Katie Steele 6
Defiance, Missouri 122, 123
Diebold, David 54
Diebold, Joseph 54
Diebold Orchards and Greenhouses 50, 54, 55
Diebold, Paula 54
Dierberg, Ellen 140
Dierberg, Jim 128
Dierberg, Mary 128
Dippenaar, Alwyn J. 92, 95
Dixon, Brandon 114
Dressel, Chuck 112
Dressel, Eva 112
Dressel, Lucian 112

E
Eagle's Nest 24, 41, 42, 43, 44
Eckenfels, Bob 96, 97
Eckenfels, Emily 96, 97
Eckenfels Farms 50, 96, 97
Eckenfels, Kayla 96, 97
Eckenfels, Matthew 96, 97
Eckenfels, Sue 96, 97
Eolia, Missouri 28
Eureka, Missouri 14

F
Family Friendly Farm 50, 62, 63
Farmington Farmers' Market 72, 73, 97
Farmington, Missouri 72, 73
Fasnacht, Darrell 62
Fasnacht, Matthew 62
Fasnacht, Rachel 62
Fennewald, Sharon 134
Fenton, Missouri 162
Fermentation Room Cafe 70, 71
Fister Farm 100, 162, 163
Fister, Fran 162
Fister, Neal 162
Fredericksburg, Missouri 150
Fritz, Mary 120
Fritz, Dr. Robert 120
Furstenau, Anna 170
Furstenau, Nathan 170
Furstenau, Nina 9, 170
Furstenau, Terry 170

G
Garth Woodside Mansion 24, 38, 39
Geisert, Ben 166
Geisert, D. John 166, 167
Geisert, Todd 166, 167
Gihring, Carson 52, 53
Gihring, Christal 52
Gihring Family Farm 50, 52, 53
Gihring, Jedidiah 52
Gihring, Leah 52, 53
Gihring, Mark 52
Gihring, Wyatt 52, 53
Gihring Family, The 9
Gilbert, Jeremy 28, 29
Gilbert, Laura 48
Gill, Clyde 22
Ginsberg, Michael 34
Ginsberg, Pam 34
Gosen, Don 140
Grapevine Grill 88, 91
Grass, Carol 116, 117
Grass, Kirk 116, 117
Gruhlke's Microbrewery 100, 116, 117, 119

H
Hagler, Jon 7
Hannibal, Missouri 8, 34, 35, 36, 37, 38, 39
Harold, Leonard 110
Haynes, Ralph 152
Heisler, Jeri 104
Heisler, Terry 104
Held, Betty 132
Held, Jim 132
Held, Jon 132
Held, Thomas 132, 133
Hemman, Al 58
Hemman, Bonnie 58, 59
Hemman, Dorothy 58, 59
Hemman, Doug 58, 59
Hemman Winery 50, 58, 59
Hermannhof Winery 100, 128, 129
Hermann, Missouri 8, 28, 124, 125, 126, 127, 128, 129, 130, 132, 133, 134, 135, 136, 137, 138, 139, 140, 141, 142, 143, 144, 146, 150, 171
Hermann Wurst Haus 100, 134, 142, 143
Herrera, Sarah 170
Herrin, Shawn 104
Hinkebein Hills Farm 50, 60, 64, 65
Hinkebein, Karlios 64
Hofherr, James 18
Hofherr, Pat 18
Hofherr, Peter 18
Holt, Elijah 140, 141
Hopen, Paul 106
Hughey, Mary 136
Hughey, Rick 136
Hurst, Janet 130, 131

I
Indian Creek Winery 24, 46, 47

J
Jackson, Missouri 52, 74, 75, 76, 77, 78, 79
Jackson, W.R.P. 46
Jameson, Gretchen 160
Janet Hurst Cheese-Making Classes 130, 131
Jefferson City, Missouri 126, 128
John G's Bier Deck 104, 105
John G's Tap Room 100, 104, 105
Johnson, Dave 132, 133
Johnson, Hank 88
Johnson, Jackie 88
Jones, Gerry 74
Jones Heritage Farms and Market 50, 60, 74, 75
Justus, James 136

K
Kansas City, Missouri 128
Keith, Connie 138
Kelso, Missouri 54
Kirksville, Missouri 130
Kiser, Rachel 46
Klondike Cafe 108

Knoernschild, Bob 110
Knoernschild Centennial Farms Shop 110
Knoernschild, Ellen 110
Kooyumjian, Tony 106, 108
Kron, Jim 94

L

Lake St. Louis Farmers' Market 45
Lambay, Adam 88, 89, 91
Lauer, Rich 146
Laughing Stalk Farmstead 50, 60, 66, 67
LeRoy, Paul 128
Les Lavandes Bed and Breakfast and Tea House 100, 158, 159
Linza, Dan 88, 89
Little Log Cabin 70
Lorch, Chris 122
Los, Joey 146
Louisiana Farmers' Market 41, 45
Louisiana, Missouri 8, 40, 41, 42, 43, 44, 45
Louisiana's Meyer Farm 40
LulaBelle's Restaurant 24, 34, 35

M

Maplewood Farmers' Market 57, 111
Marthasville, Missouri 144
McKaskle Family Farm 62
McKittrick Mercantile 100, 146, 147
McKittrick, Missouri 146, 147
Meier Horse Shoe Pines 50, 76, 77
Meier, Steve 76
Meier, Teresa 76
Meiser, Dennis 12
Meiser, Fern 12, 31
Meramec River 8, 11, 22
Meyer, Charlie 44, 45
Meyer Farms 24, 42, 44, 45
Meyer, Jerry 152
Meyer, Peggy 44, 45
Miller, Becky 122
Miller, Ken 122
Miller, Sidney 138
Mississippi River 8, 25, 32, 34, 42, 48, 51, 58, 70
Missouri Governor's Cup 18, 106, 114, 132
Missouri Hick Bar-B-Q 10, 12, 13
Missouri River 7, 8, 101, 104, 108, 112, 122, 128, 144, 146, 150, 152, 166
Moberly, Missouri 28
Moeser, Paul 102
Monroe City, Missouri 46, 47
Montelle Winery 100, 106, 108, 109
Montgomery City, Missouri 48, 49
Morrison, Missouri 8, 148, 149, 150, 151
Mount Pleasant Winery 100, 112, 113
Mueller, Beth 154
Mueller, Jerry 154, 155
Mueller, Lois 154, 155
Mueller, Mary 154
Mueller, Robert 154, 155
Mueller, Sue 154
Muench, Frederick 112
Muench, George 112
Mundwiller, Becca 134
Mundwiller, Deana 134
Mundwiller, Liz 134

N

Nathe, Deborah 14
Nathe, Steve 14
National Register of Historic Places 128, 132
Newbold, Chris 114
New Haven, Missouri 116, 152, 153, 154, 155, 156, 157
Niman Ranch 166
Noboleis Vineyards 100, 114, 115
Nolan, Lou Ann 114
Nolan, Robert 114
Norv's Meat Shop 168
Nott, Katie 22

O

Osbourne, John 46
Osbourne, Sheila 46
Overlook Farm 24, 32, 33

P

Peaceful Bend Vineyard 10, 22, 23
Pennington, Colin 112
Perryville, Missouri 80, 81, 82, 83
Peterson, Ross 66
Pettus, Nathalie 32, 33
Pettus, William G. 32
Phillips, Natasha 141
Pinckney Bend Distillery 100, 152, 153
Pioneer Apple Orchards 50, 78
Polcyn, Mike 33
Portwood, April 26
Portwood, Laura 26
Preckshot, Geoffrey 46
Prohibition 7, 18, 110, 112, 124, 126, 128, 132, 150
Puchta, Adam 124
Puchta, Randolph 124
Puchta, Tim 124

R

Rackheath House 32
Radtke, Marge 133
Ricky's Chocolate Box 100, 136, 137
Ritter Hills 60
River Hills Elderberry Producers 126
River Ridge Winery 50, 70, 71
River's Edge Restaurant 100, 150, 151
Robey, John D. 46
Röbller Vineyard and Winery 100, 154, 155
Rolling Meadows Vineyard and Winery 100, 160, 161
Rolsen, John 38, 39
Rolsen, Julie 38, 39
Rose Bed Inn 50, 68, 69
Rose Water Spa 68
Route 66 Fudge Shop 10, 16, 17
Russell, Jack 86
Russell, Joal 86

S

Saballa, Tony 86, 87
Sassafras Valley Farm 100, 148, 149
Saugrain, Antoine 32
Schaaf, DeWayne 60, 61
Scheffer, Janet 20
Scheffer, Sybill 20
Scheffer, Tom 20
Schmidt, Kelsey 16
Schulte Bakery 100, 164, 165
Scifers, Emily 66
Second Shift Brewing 100, 156, 157
Sederwalls Family, The 8
Sederwalls, Howard 36
Sederwalls, Velma 36
Simmons, Linda 150
Simmons on the Waterfront 150
Simmons, Steve 150
Slater, Vicki 134, 135
Sloan, Bill 134, 135
Sloan, Lynette 142, 143
Sloan, Mike 142, 143
Smith, Jerry 70, 71
Smith, Joannie 70, 71
Soulard Market 57, 97
Starkenburg, Missouri 158, 159
Station Restaurant, The 32
Staude, Claudia 160
Staude, Ed 160
St. Charles, Missouri 40
Steelville, Missouri 12, 13, 22, 23
Ste. Genevieve, Missouri 84, 85, 86, 87, 88, 91, 95, 96, 97, 98, 91
Steinberg, Kaitlin 152
St. James, Missouri 8, 18, 19, 20, 21
St. James Winery 10, 18, 19
St. Louis, Missouri 3, 8, 25, 28, 44, 51, 64, 74, 88, 89, 97, 98, 110, 122, 128, 144, 162, 168
St. Mary, Missouri 86, 98, 99
Stoeckley, John 42
Stoeckley, Karen 42
Stone Hill Winery 100, 132, 133
Stonie's Sausage Shop 50, 82, 83
Strussion, Marty 84, 85
Strussion, Mary Jo 84, 85
St. Vincent's In-the-Vineyard 89
Sugar and Spice Laura's Delights 24, 48, 49
Sugar Creek Vineyards and Winery 100, 122, 123
Sullivan, Missouri 134
Swiss Meat and Sausage Company 100, 134, 135, 142
Sybill's St. James 10, 20, 21

T

The Cottage 100, 138, 139
Thierbach, Ed 144, 145
Thierbach, Elise 144, 145
Thierbach, LaVerda 144, 145
Thierbach Market 145
Thierbach Orchards and Berry Farm 9, 100, 144, 145
Thierbach, Otto 144, 145
Thierbach, Susie 144, 145
Thierbach, Wesley 144, 145
Thomas, Janice 134
Thomas, Judy 164
Thomas, Leo 164
Thomas, Paul 164
Tin Mill Brewery 100, 140, 141
Todd Geisert Farms 100, 166, 167
Tower Grove Farmers' Market 57, 111

V

Vintage Restaurant 132
Vogt, Tom 32

W

Warrenton, Missouri 160, 161
Washington, Missouri 104, 110, 162, 163, 164, 165, 166, 167, 168, 169
Washington University Market 57
Weber, Myrta 158
Weber, Richard 158
Webster Grove Market 57
Weston, Martha 40, 41
Wibbenmeyer, Barb 83
Wibbenmeyer, Dane 82
Wibbenmeyer, Don 82
Wibbenmeyer, Roger 82, 83
Wibbenmeyer, Stanislaus (Stonie) 82
Wibbenmeyer, Tyson 82, 83
Wibbenmeyer, Zoey 82
Williams, Brian 168
Williams Brothers Meats 9, 100, 168, 169
Williams, Christopher 168
Williams, Dan 168
Williams, Leonard 72
Williams, Linda 72, 73
Williams, Steve 168, 169
Wilson, Grace 16
Wilson, Marcia 16
Winding Brook Estate 10, 14, 15
Windrush Farm 50, 72, 73
Windy Hill Cut Flower Farm 100, 120, 121
Woods, Ed 30
Woods, Regina 30
Woods Smoked Meats 24, 30, 31
Wright, Joyce 126
Wright, Tim 126, 127

Attractions & Specialty Items

Art Gallery 68, 138
Bed and Breakfast 34, 42, 58, 68, 86, 146, 148, 152, 158
Biscotti Bar 84
Butterfly Garden 98
Catering 60, 64, 104, 146
Cheese-Making Class 130, 146
Cherry Orchard 144
Christmas Shop 76
Christmas Trees 76
Clothing and Accessories 80
Community Supported Agriculture 66, 111
Custom Wine Bottles 46
Eden Trail 160
Felting Class 146
Floral Arrangements 120
Floral Gardens 84
Flowers, Plants and Seeds 54, 72, 120
Geese and Ducks 148
Gift Boxes and Baskets 78, 82
Gift Shop 14, 20, 106, 112, 154
Goldfish Pond 68
Hayrides 110, 144
Hickory Pit BBQ and Catering Food Truck 64
Home-Garden Menu 102
Horse and Carriage Ride 76
Katy Bike Trail 104
Lavender 14, 44, 158, 162
Limestone Cavern 84
Live Music 22, 58, 70, 105, 106, 112, 114, 132, 154
Lodging 34, 42, 58, 68, 70, 86, 92, 128, 146, 148, 152, 158
Maze 78
Meat Processing 30, 42, 82, 168
Nut Cracking 54
Petting Zoo 144
Pick Your Own 78, 79, 144, 166
Picnics 84
Salon and Spa 68
Seasonal Menu 60, 74, 88, 114, 138
Seasonal Treats 136
Self-Service Roadside Produce 166
Soil Enhancers 72
Tasting Room 46, 84, 86, 87, 88, 106, 107, 108, 109, 112, 114, 115, 128, 154, 156, 157, 160
Tilapia Fisheries 32
Yarn 80, 162
Wedding Flowers 120
Wiener Schnitzel 102, 132

Specialty Foods

Antibiotic- and Hormone-Free Meats 64, 74, 166
Apple Butter 62, 78, 110
Apple Cider 54, 144
Artisan Cheese 56, 130
Baetje Farms Goat Cheese (Plain, Three-Pepper and Garlic and Chives) 57
Bamboo Partridge 36
Black Angus Beef Cattle 92
Bloomsdale Cheese 56
Cajun-Creole 150
Cherbourg Cheese 56
Danish 48
Deer Sausage 30
Dehydrated Produce 72
Donuts 48, 164
Fasnachts Fresh Cow's Milk 62
Fleur de la Vallee Cheese 56
Fresh Bread Loaves 164
Freshly Baked Bread 84
Fresh Produce 44, 54, 62, 72, 74, 78, 98, 110, 126, 144, 166
Fried Tomatoes 102, 138
German Springerles 48
Goat Cheese 56, 130
Goat Milk 162
Grass-Fed Animals 62
Grass-Fed Beef 62, 96
Handmade Pasta 60
Heirloom Tomato Powder 72
Herbs and Spices 72, 82, 110, 120, 166
Hinkebein Hills' Meats 64
Homemade Pies 48, 54, 78, 164
Honey 40, 62, 110
Hormone-Free Eggs 74
Kochkaese Cheese 130
Lavender Cookies 158
Lavender Ice Cream 158
Linden Tea 158
Marinades 82
Missouri Cedar Smoked Bar-B-Que 12
Norv's Smoked Summer Sausage 168
Old Fashioned Fudge 16
Old-Fashioned Turtles 26
Olive-Oil Soap 162
Organic Food and Produce 32, 66, 72
Organic Rice 62
Pastured Lamb 76
Peggy Meyer's Granola Muffins 44
Pickles 142
Popcorn 62
Preserves, Jellies and Jams 110, 126, 134, 142
Pumpkins/Pumpkin Patch 78, 110, 166
Quail 36
Ricky's Chocolate Truffles 136
Ricky's Cream Frankenstein Heads 136
Ricky's Marshmallow Eyeball Cookies 136
Ricky's Spotted Turtle 136
River's Edge Orange Cajun Sauce 150
River's Edge Raspberry Jazz 150
River's Edge Sizzlin' Pepper Sauce 150
River's Edge Sweet-and-Sour Salad Dressing 150
Route 66 Candy Bars 16
Seafood 150
Sheep's Milk Cheese 56
Specialty Baby Cakes 16
Specialty Meats 30, 64, 82, 134, 142, 148, 166, 168
Stonie's Hickory Smoked Bacon 83
Stonie's Rosemary Basil Thyme Seasoning 83
Summer Sausage 30, 82, 134, 142, 168
Sweet Betsy Smoked Ham 31
Sweet Betsy from Pike Products 30
Swiss Meat and Sausage Swiss Signature Brats 134
Swiss Meat Maple Syrup Breakfast Sausage 135
Syrup 52, 110
Tasty Toms Tomatoes 98
The Cottage Prime Rib 138
The Old Homestead Brand Products 162
Thibodeau Cheese 56
Vegetable Stand 98, 99
Wedding Cakes 48
Williams Brothers Apple Cinnamon Bratwurst 168
Williams Brothers Kentucky Bourbon Bratwurst 168
Williams Brothers Mediterranean Bratwurst 168

Events

Autumn at Peaceful Bend 22
Barbecue and Chili Cook-Off 116
Big Band Dance 132
Cajun Concert on the Hill 132
Croquet Tournaments 116
Dancing 146
Easter Egg Hunt 116
European High Tea 158
Farm-to-Table Events 32
Festival Weekends 119
First Friday Art Show 68
Garth Mansion Private Tours 38
International Dinner Events 138
Kimmswick's Strawberry Festival 110
Lavender and Libations 14
Lavender Tea Luncheons 14
Lucy Days Grape Stomping 58
Maifest 132
Monster Bike Bash 104
Nature Trail Scavenger Hunt 116
October Beer Fest 104
Oktoberfest 132
Old Fashioned Christmas Walk 58
Shiver Fest 104
Tasting of Missouri Wine Weekends 38
Wine Trail Event 116, 132

Beer and Wine

Adam Puchta
  Hunter's Red 125
  Nortons 124
  Sherry 124
  Vignoles 124
Augusta Brewing
  Hyde Park Stout 104
  Norton 106, 107
Augusta Winery
  Vignoles 106
Bat Creek
  Flip Nut 28
  Gold Reserve 28
  Heartland Wheat 28
  Machine Shed Stout 28, 29
  Midwest Farmer's Daughter Ale 28, 29
  Pike County Pale 28
  Platinum Reserve 28
  Silver Reserve 28
Bias
  Apple Weisser Flieder 119
  Chambourcin 116
  DeChaunac 116
  Norton 116
  Strawberry Weisser Flieder 116, 118
Charleville
  Barrel Fermented Chardonel 87
Chaumette
  Chambourcin 91
Craft Beers 12, 92, 104, 117, 140, 156
Crown Valley Brewery
  Plowboy Porter 94
Crown Valley Winery
  Chardonel 92
  Riesling 93
  Velvet Muscat 92
Flavored Brandy 108
Gruhlke's Microbrewery
  Black Lager 117
  Chubby Stout 117
  Done Did It Dortmunder 117
  Gruhlke's Light 117
  Gruhlke's Wheat 117
  Nate's Belgian Tripel 117
  Naughty's Ale 117
  Opa Willy's Homemade Rootbeer 117
  India Pale Ale 117
Hemman
  Blackberry Wine 58, 59
  Cushaw (Squash) Wine 58
  Pumpkin Wine 58
  Rhubarb Wine 58
Indian Creek
  Blackberry Wine 46
  Norton 46
  Peach Wine 46
  Pirate's Gold 46
  Riesling 46
  Strawberry Wine 46
  Sweet Cherry Wine 46
  Vignoles 46